Endorsements

Keith Zafren is an inspiring guide on this adventure into the heart of fathering. Read this book. It will make you a better dad, and it may even help you forgive your own father for the mistakes he inevitably made.

— Neil Chethik
Executive Director, The Carnegie Center for Literacy and Learning
Author of *FatherLoss* and *VoiceMale*

If you want a trustworthy, trail-worn guide into wise, effective, and fulfilling fathering, then look no further. In addition to surveying fatherhood literature and research, Keith Zafren candidly shares his wound of being abandoned by his father, the growth he experienced being mentored by great dads, the inspiration he discovered coaching the sons of absentee fathers in prison, and the healing he has found loving and affirming his own children. As to a great trail guide, you'll come back to him again and again for wisdom and encouragement.

— Graham Scharf
Author of *The Apprenticeship of Being Human:
Why Early Childhood Parenting Matters to Everyone*

I am not even the primary audience for this book, and yet, I was moved to tears numerous times; it gave me a new perspective on my own wounds—having lost my biological father five weeks before I was born—and it showed me how I can be a better mother to my two adult stepchildren. The content is relevant and timely, and Keith provides an answer to a problem that has the potential to profoundly impact the world by modeling and teaching how to transform non-love into love. What could be better than that?

— Jennifer Read Hawthorne
International speaker, award-winning and
bestselling author and editor

WOW!!! "Healing a Father Wound" was by far the most impactful and emotional section of any book I have ever read. I can't even describe how deeply this teaching affected me.

The feeling of "choked up" stayed throughout reading the section and keeps coming back even now. I realized clearly how my own father wound has affected my entire life—and still does to this day. It also made me realize how the healing process is a daily reward to me and my boys, and so worth the effort. My heart was smiling while my eyes filled with tears. Awesome book!

— Patrick McMillan
Founder, TeachingHappiness.com
Author, *An Exercise in Happiness for Kids*

Being in the presence of Keith's writing is like being perched over an intimate cup of tea with a perceptive and wise friend. With intuitive mastery, Keith attends to his topic with authenticity and alacrity. Though I'm not a father, I do have one. I'm not a son, but I mother three of them. Finally, there is a book—a guide of sorts—illustrating what thoughtful fathering actually looks like with real-life, raw, human examples of his own and others. This work is as practical as it is deeply soulful. Through his own compelling self-observation and personal disclosure, it is obvious that Keith has steeped in and skillfully examined his own human and humbling experience of both parenting and being parented. This enabled me to trust him and allowed me to trust myself in taking his life lessons to heart. In particular, Keith's masterful, gentle section on healing a father wound and grief allowed me to begin to navigate an aching part of my own life. What a nourishing read for me as I make sense of how I was fathered, what my boys are seeking in their dad, and how I can come alongside my husband in co-parenting our children with a new comprehension and compassion.

— Susan Olesek
International Enneagram Facilitator and Coach
Founder, The Enneagram Prison Project

Unfortunately, I've made some foolish choices and served a six-year term in prison. Just this past week, I was granted the blessing of sweet freedom. Although I was heartbroken and utterly devastated over not being able to be the dad I needed to be and for causing pain in my children's precious lives, my prison sentence ended up being the best thing that ever happened to me. Keith Zafren taught me to become a much better father from behind prison walls. I learned how I have been affected by not having a father and how to ensure that I do not inflict the same deep wounds upon my children. This book will help many men become the dads we all want to be, teach us how to lovingly affirm our children, and provide healing from whatever wounds we may have experienced from inadequate fathering when we were young.

— Bobby Colombo
Formerly Incarcerated Father
Member of Class IX of the Prison Entrepreneurship Program

I have had the good fortune of working as a business partner with Keith for the last three years. Seeing firsthand how he raises his sons and how he handles his life and business is a daily reminder to me to not only be the best dad I can be but also the best person I can be. He is such a genuine man. His passion for helping people is unsurpassed by anyone I know.

— Jeff Boswell
Operations Manager, My Three Sons Professional Painting

I had already been mentored by Keith Zafren for several years when I founded the Prison Entrepreneurship Program (PEP) in Texas. Keith was the single most influential person in my life who shaped me into the leader and spiritual person I am today. He served as a founding member of our governing board and coached me through many of our challenging start-up issues.

Starting in our second class, I knew we needed a strong male/father role model for our men. It would have been easier to have someone local fill this role, but I was committed to providing our participants with world-class teachers and mentors, so we invested in flying Keith from Kentucky, eventually on a monthly basis, to teach on fatherhood and spirituality. He became a Character Formation Coach and deeply impacted our men's lives as they learned to become honorable men and great dads. Keith's influence and involvement with PEP was definitely one of the best aspects of the entire program. I witnessed our participants' transformation firsthand.

Keith remains a great friend and advisor to me. I'm honored he's serving on the National Advisory Board for Defy Ventures, my second nonprofit in the prison rehabilitation sector. I couldn't be more excited about what he's creating with The Great Dads Project. Keith is a tremendously gifted teacher. He may be the most devoted father I've ever met. The Great Dads Project is filling a tremendous unmet need. I believe the key to restoring the most broken communities in America is to equip men to be great fathers. Keith is perfectly equipped through his life and professional experiences to lead this movement.

— Catherine Rohr
Founder and former CEO, The Prison Entrepreneurship Program
Founder and current CEO, Defy Ventures
www.defyventures.org

Reading Keith's book was truly a transformative experience. Told through compelling and artistically crafted narrative, *How to Be a Great Dad* offers a deeply soulful awakening while providing a practical guide to being the dad every father desires to be. It doesn't matter where you are in your journey or what your relationship with your own father has been, Keith reminds you that it is never too late to heal, or to learn to transform pain into joy.

— Dr. Lori Friesen
Animal-Assisted Literacy Expert and Speaker
Author, *The Beginning Teacher's Handbook for Elementary School*

Special Endorsements

Our dad takes us on one-on-one trips on our birthdays. He spends as much time with us as he can. I like that he tucks us in at night. My dad is a really good dad and I like being around him.

— JD Zafren
Age 15

Our dad is a great father to us. He unselfishly spends lots of time with each one of us. And he has been helping fathers around the world become great dads. I love him.

— Cal Zafren
Age 13

You should read my dad's book to become a better dad. I'm not saying that you're a bad dad, but you can always get better, even my dad can, and he is a great dad. He wants to help you, me, and everyone else he can.

— Kai Zafren
Age 11

With Gratitude

SIR JOHN HUNT, who scaled Mount Everest in 1953, wrote, "The ascent of Everest was not the work of one day, nor even of those few unforgettable weeks in which we climbed . . . It is, in fact, a tale of sustained and tenacious endeavor by many, over a long period of time." Producing a great book is somewhat akin to that experience; it takes an incredibly diverse and specially gifted team to do so. I have many for whom I am thankful.

First, I am grateful for my dad. Although there were holes left in my heart from ways in which I didn't get enough from him, he was also one of my great teachers. It is out of the ashes of my relationship with my dad that something good has arisen. I am a better man today as a result of all I've worked through and learned to accept, compassionately embrace, and forgive. I am a much better dad to my three sons because of my dad's fathering of me, incomplete as it was. And I have a lifework before me as a direct result of my father's influence in my life. Dad, I do love you and thank you for giving me life, loving me as you were able, and gifting me with the pain that has become passion. I'm thankful you were my dad.

Jack Canfield has been a long-time mentor to me through his writing, speaking, and example. I am thrilled that he has taken an interest in my work and has been so supportive. Thank you, Jack, for all you have taught me, the way you continue to instruct, inspire, and empower me, and for writing the foreword to my first book.

Two longtime friends became partners in The Great Dads Project when it was just a vision in my mind. When I first explained what I hoped to give to men everywhere, David Haug spoke words to me I will never forget, "That could change the world," and Jerry Hall said, "This is what you were made for." When the three of us met to dream about what this project could become, David and Jerry both said, "Before you do anything else, you need to write a book." Without the support, encouragement, challenge, and love of these two friends, this book would not exist. Thank you, David and Jerry. I believe we are better friends and that each of us is a better dad today as a result of our work together the last two years.

Once I finished the first draft of my manuscript, I asked numerous mentors and friends to read it and provide feedback. That feedback was crucial in shaping the book you now have in your hands. I am grateful to those who helped me write this book in this way. Thank you (in alphabetical order) to Elizabeth Anthony-Dershimer, Angela Anderson, Brenda Bartella Peterson, Mike Bauer, Geoffrey Berwind, Neil Chethik, Jerry Hall, David Haug, Jim Kenney, Jon Lachelt, Mark Manley, Bill and Molly Meyer, Susan Olesek, Bob Peterson, and Graham Scharf.

Special thanks to my friend and fellow author, Graham Scharf. Graham's careful reading of my multiple drafts, his in-depth and insightful feedback, his relentless encouragement and creative ideas, and his seemingly tireless spirit and remarkable list of resources were a constant source of strength and creativity for me. I can't thank you enough, Graham. This is a much better book because of you. Thank you also for your written contributions to it.

Patrick McMillan, a dear friend and fellow dad and author, was a regular source of encouragement, one of my cheerleaders, and a valuable contributor to this book. Thank you, Patrick.

Catherine Hamrick, my professional copy editor, was remarkable. I learned so much about writing, grammar, syntax, and all those other important English tools I failed to master in college by carefully reading and sometimes agonizing over her repeated and relentless feedback. She read and revised my manuscript three times! Thank you, Catherine; you deserve sainthood. (Is it okay to use a semicolon in that sentence?)

From my fantastic writing instructors and course mates at the Carnegie Center for Literacy and Learning, I learned so much. I am especially grateful to Neil Chethik, Leatha Kendrick, Brenda Bartella Peterson, and Angela Anderson for their detailed feedback that led to significant structural changes in my manuscript and helped me find and trust "my voice," tell more stories, and eliminate my academic style of writing left over from Ph.D. work. I am so thankful now, as all my readers will be!

Steve Harrison and his remarkable team at Quantum Leap Publicity Training tremendously helped me to shape my message, think clearly about my audience, and trained me to get that message out. Steve gave me the seed idea for The Great Dad Challenge. I am particularly grateful to senior coach Geoffrey Berwind and media specialist Raia King.

Much thanks to the remarkable team of creative people at 1106 Design. Working with each of the experts on their team was a delight. They held my hand through each step of the creative process of cover design, interior layout, proofreading, and all the many details to bring my first book to publication. I appreciate especially the careful and knowledgeable feedback from my project manager there, Ronda Rawlins, and from Michelle DeFilippo, the owner of the company. Thank you, ladies. I tried to make the content of the book worthwhile, but you presented it beautifully. I'm delighted with the final product.

I am so grateful for my wonderful boys, and all the love, joy, laughter, and wonder we share together. I love being a dad and am so grateful for the life I live with my remarkable boys. I am grateful for JD, my first-born son, and the young man he is becoming. I am thankful for Cal, my second-born, and all in life he is achieving. And I am so grateful for Kai, my youngest little guy, and the joy he brings to life. I give thanks for all we share and all we are continuing to build together. Without you remarkable young men, this father would never be the dad I am today and this book would not exist. Thank you!

And I am grateful for Debbie, the mother of our children. I'm grateful that raising our beautiful three boys together helped me become the dad I am today, and that we were both dedicated to being the best parents we could be. She always has been and continues to be a very loving and dedicated mom.

HOW
to Be a
GREAT
DAD

NO MATTER
WHAT KIND
OF FATHER
YOU HAD

KEITH ZAFREN

How to Be a Great Dad—No Matter What Kind of Father You Had

For information about this title or to order other books and/or electronic media, contact the publisher:

Peak Communications and Publishing
1067 North Main St. #131
Nicholasville, KY 40356
info@peakcommunicationspress.com

ISBNs:
978-0-9857138-1-2 Print/Softcover
978-0-9857138-2-9 eBook

Printed in the United States of America

Cover and Interior design: 1106 Design

Author photo: Melissa Dondero

Dedication

To JD, Cal, and Kai,
my three sons.

You are the beautiful, healing gifts of my life.

And to the courageous men of the
Prison Entrepreneurship Program
who rebuilt their lives as fathers
and birthed in me the vision for
The Great Dads Project.

Thank you.
My six years with you were a gift of inspiration.

Table of Contents

Foreword

By Jack Canfield

O N FIRST MEETING Keith Zafren, I immediately felt a strong connection to him, his work with The Great Dads Project, and the book he had written about it. Because my life purpose is to inspire and empower people to live their highest vision in a context of love and joy, in harmony with the highest good of all concerned, I immediately related to what Keith was aspiring to accomplish. I believe Keith's message is very important. I enthusiastically support him in his efforts to reach out to men everywhere, to help them heal and grow to become the great dads they long to be and their children so desperately need them to be.

We all know how easy it is, biologically, to become a father. What we often don't realize is that it takes work, dedication, and learned skills to become a dad, especially a great dad.

My father was an alcoholic and often physically and emotionally abusive. My mother divorced him when I was only six years old in order to protect my two brothers and me from my dad. I did not have an early example of what a great dad looked like and how he fathered children. Years later, when I became a father, I loved my sons deeply, but I didn't know how to fully demonstrate my love because of my experience with my father. I didn't know how to be close to my sons the way I wanted to be or to father them the way they needed me to. I spent many years recovering from and healing the wounds left in my psyche by these experiences. So have my sons. I wish, as a younger father, I had discovered the material Keith now teaches to guide me toward becoming the great dad I longed to be and healing the deep wounds that prevented me from doing so.

Like me, Keith experienced deep wounding from an inadequate relationship with his father. Like me, he did not know how to effectively father his own children at first. And like me, he is committed to his own personal development and human potential, as well as his vision to make a positive difference in the world by bringing healing to others and helping them achieve their dreams. In his case, Keith longs to transform all fathers into great dads by inspiring and empowering men to become their best selves and to make a significant and positive impact on their children.

Although you might be successful in your business or your vocation, your success as a dad is far more important because it affects not only you but also your children, and ultimately generation upon generation to come. And yet most men spend very little time pondering the question, *Am I doing the right things to become a great dad?*

How to Be a Great Dad addresses this most important question in a profound way. It's filled with personal stories, focused on powerful principles, and written for real people. It's written for fathers like me who have wounds to be healed, as well as for men who have enjoyed the loving affirmation of a great father but have discovered it's not so easy to be one themselves. This book is also useful if you do not yet have children because it will help you better understand the impact your father had on you. Keith's story, like mine, is one of pain and abandonment, yet the hope and example he offers are beautiful and compelling.

Written with insight, wisdom, and engaging humor, *How to Be a Great Dad* is far more than Keith's personal story. Grounded upon solid research, commentary by leading experts, and real-life examples, it compassionately and concretely walks you step by step down the path to effective and fulfilling fathering. In a very compelling way, it will teach you how to positively impact your children while at the same time guide you through a profound and effective healing process from any wounds left in your soul by your own father.

Even if you feel challenged being a dad because your father did not fully love, affirm, or accept you, you *can* heal from neglect, lack of loving expression, or even abandonment. In seeking your own healing from your father wounds, you will find the freedom to create strong, lasting bonds with your children and a more intimate, satisfying relationship with your partner.

Please be assured that if you need to repair a damaged relationship with a child, it's never too late. Keith will show you how. You have the ability to become a part of a new generation of fathers who will change the world by impacting not only your children but also your children's children—and their children.

To keep you inspired and taking action, Keith has included an epilogue comprised of additional real-life fathering stories similar to those that fill the pages of the *Chicken Soup for the Soul*® books. I'm sure you'll love and benefit from these stories as much as I have.

After you read this book, I hope you'll share several copies with other men in your life who might need to read it and who will benefit from what it teaches. Discuss what you are learning with other fathers. Create support groups. Admit your mistakes and celebrate your victories. Encourage one another in your fathering efforts. Cheer one another on.

Allow Keith to teach you how to live your highest vision of fathering in the context of love and joy for your own highest good, your children's, and the world's.

Jack Canfield
Santa Barbara, CA
December 2012

Jack Canfield, America's #1 Success Coach, is the co-creator of the billion-dollar book brand *Chicken Soup for the Soul®* and a leading authority on Peak Performance and Life Success. The *Chicken Soup* series now has more than 200 titles, including *Chicken Soup for the Father's Soul, Chicken Soup for the Soul: Dads and Daughters,* and *Chicken Soup for the Father and Son Soul. Chicken Soup* titles have sold more than 500 million copies in over forty languages worldwide. Canfield has authored, coauthored, and edited forty-seven *New York Times* bestsellers. He is also the founder of The Canfield Training Group and the Transformational Leadership Council. www.jackcanfield.com

---

Synopsis

*H*ow to Be a Great Dad can radically improve your relationship with your kids, no matter what you feel you didn't get from your own dad or how you think you may have fallen short so far—or even failed—in being the dad you want to be. It's an essential read for men who are not yet dads but hope or plan to be one day.

Moms will love this book because it offers the men in their lives inspiration and loads of practical ideas to help them become a great dad to their kids. It will also help moms better understand their relationship with their own father.

Here's What You Can Expect
Section One, *Three Crucial Fathering Skills,* explains and illustrates with great stories three essential actions you can take with and for your children to set them up for success in every area of their lives as they grow up. These chapters show you how to provide a fantastic foundation for their belief in themselves, what they imagine they deserve by way of personal friendships and intimate relationships, and what they think they can or cannot accomplish in the world. Your

fathering makes a profound difference. You can do this. This section shows you how and inspires you to action.

Section Two, *Healing a Father Wound,* invites you to take a closer look at your relationship with your own father. These chapters show you how issues from the past with your father might be limiting your ability to become the great dad you long to be now. Many men don't realize that their feelings of inadequacy or their lack of fathering skills often stem from a poor experience with or a lack of closeness to their own fathers. I had a painful experience with my father. I tell my personal story in this section about my wounded heart and psyche, how my father wound crippled my ability to form and sustain an intimate relationship with a woman, and how my ongoing healing journey set me free to become the dad I always wished I'd had. You will find clear and practical steps to help you face, embrace, and heal from whatever wound you may have experienced growing up.

Section Three is all about *Taking Action,* making the inspiration and practical suggestions offered throughout the book stick. This section focuses on what it takes to move from good information to real transformation and makes it realistic and achievable.

The Epilogue, *It's Worth It!,* offers a series of real-life dad stories that show how dads are living into the skills and suggestions offered in this book. These men are becoming effective and fulfilled dads and they're experiencing great results and closeness with their kids. Their stories are inspiring to us because they are real and attainable.

Know that *Great Dads Shape Great Kids.* This book will show you how, step by step, even if you don't know what to do to be a great dad or if you didn't experience one yourself. I look forward to hearing your story soon. Enjoy!

Keith Zafren
Founder, The Great Dads Project

Introduction

GREAT FATHERING can change the world. And Lord knows we need it. The world in which we are trying to raise our children is much more complex and challenging than the world in which we were raised. Twenty-four million children (one child in three) will go to bed tonight in a home where there is no father. Nearly 80 percent of the crimes and social ills we face, including teen pregnancy, poverty, and drug and alcohol abuse, trace back to fatherlessness or inadequate fathering.

On the other hand, children who have been consistently affirmed, who know they will never be rejected, and who feel deeply loved have the best chance of growing into mature, responsible, passionate adults who develop their own vibrant vision for contributing to the highest good of the world.

Children with involved fathers display:

- ▸ Better cognitive outcomes even as infants.
- ▸ Higher self-esteem and less depression as teenagers.
- ▸ Higher grades, test scores, and overall academic achievement.
- ▸ Lower levels of drug and alcohol use.
- ▸ Higher levels of empathy and other pro-social behavior.

Great fathering makes a profound difference for children. It also makes a big difference for fathers—and for society. That's what this book is about. It will inspire and empower you to become a dad who knows how to demonstrate your love for your kids in a way that promotes the greatest and most positive impact on many levels.

Although the primary audience for *How to Be a Great Dad* is men who are currently raising children, or soon will be, the book actually presents a universal message for all men—and women— since every one of us had fathers and many of us did not have the fathers we wish we had. That is, most people I've met around the world need some measure of the healing presented in this book and for the specific issue upon which I focus—healing a father wound. This is true for women, and it is true for men whether they end up becoming fathers or not.

For twenty-three years, I was a pastor of Christian churches, the last eight of which I served as the lead pastor of The River Church Community in San José, California, a church I founded in 1997. I was also a founding board member and a fatherhood trainer for The Prison Entrepreneurship Program (PEP) based in Houston, Texas.

In my role as a PEP trainer over a six-year period, I coached 600 men, most of whom had abandoned their children or had very little relationship with them. As a result of this work with incarcerated fathers, nearly 2,000 children received their father's loving affirmation and acceptance, many of them for the first time. Through this book, I am now bringing to men everywhere the transformative and healing teaching I shared with the men of PEP. I'll share more about PEP and some of my remarkable experiences there later.

Like many fathers today, I never built a strong bond with my own dad. In *How to Be a Great Dad*, I honestly recount the agonizing times my father walked out on our relationship and the years of self-searching it took for me to substantially heal. Along the way, I discovered how to deal with the psychological repercussions of my *father loss* and to embrace the belief that I could parent with passion, consistency, action, and abiding, nonjudgmental love and affection. You can do this too. This book will teach you how.

For Female Readers

For female readers, this will prove to be an intriguing and revealing book. There are at least two ways that this book may be enlightening. The first is in your translation of what I share with men to your own relationship with your father. Millions of women suffer the consequences of a father-wounded soul. I will address this issue in brief. The second is that you may find clues in these chapters to questions you ask, perceptions that trouble you, or experiences you've had with the men in your life that confuse you—particularly if you've had or now have an intimate relationship with a man whose father wounded him. *How to Be a Great Dad* will help you better understand him, make sense of some of the characteristics and behaviors you observe and experience, and discern ways you might help him heal and become the man and father he longs to be. A female friend who read an early version of this book wrote:

> Although I have always had a wonderful relationship with my dad, this book profoundly influenced me, a woman, helping me to understand how I might approach our relationship with more compassion, joy, and deep love. I developed a renewed appreciation for my dad's rare and wonderful ability to offer me verbal affirmation, unconditional acceptance, and physical affection.

> I did not expect to be so enlightened about my relationship with my husband. I don't think his father ever told him that he was proud of him, made him feel as though he was ever good enough, or gave him hugs or any form of spoken or physical affection—and that painfully translated into our relationship. Like his father, my husband provides

well for our family financially, but the "love, laughter, and playful moments of connection and affection" that Keith highlights children crave from their fathers—and that women crave from their husbands—is sadly lacking in many relationships.

Keith explains the deep and profound hunger for affirmation, acceptance, and affection not only present between fathers and their children, but also why it is an unfulfilled need in so many marriages.

You may find resources designed specifically for women at my website www.thegreatdadsproject.org/resources/forwomen.

A Groundswell of Change

Millions of fathers now long for the fulfillment of feeling close to their children. Though many of us approach our transition to fatherhood with enthusiasm, we also tend to feel a bit disoriented and sometimes scared. We desire to be the best dads we can be, yet we sometimes find ourselves drawing upon a vacuum of personal knowledge and experience (such as changing a diaper or bathing or burping an infant) and a cultural morass of father definitions (such as financial provider, family protector, disciplinarian, problem solver, and coach).[1]

Some of us struggle with a lack of modeling or, in some cases, poor modeling from our own dads. Many men know the consequences, sometimes the pain, left by dads who were not involved. Lots of our dads were good, faithful financial providers. For that we can be grateful. Some of them were great dads. Yet many of us wish our fathers had provided in personal ways, as well as financial. We aspire to that now: to provide more than money—if we are the financial providers for our families. We want to provide ourselves in relationship—to share love, laughter, and playful moments of connection and affection with our children.

When I write about children, I do not only mean those who share our DNA. I refer also to the children we adopt, embrace through marriage, or other children for whom we fulfill a father-figure role, such as the fatherless friend of one of our children, the child of a sister who is now a single mom, or a child for whom we serve as a Big Brother. Perhaps there is a child on an athletic team or in a social or faith community of which we are a part who has no dad. The stories and practices I share apply to all these special relationships.

What Lies Ahead?

How to Be a Great Dad is about how profoundly your fathering impacts your children for their entire lives. It's also about how fulfilling it feels to become the great dad you long to be. This book illustrates and celebrates three crucial fathering skills—affirming, accepting, and being affectionate with your children—as well as seeking your own healing where a lack of love from your father left wounds.

I share my own personal stories with you in the pages that follow. I hope my stories and those of others will show how inadequate fathering from our fathers is a common problem among men and how healing is not only possible but is also a freeing and empowering experience that enables you to give to your children the love and affirmation you may not have received. In the process, you will find further healing for your own wounded heart while strengthening your children and creating a lifelong bond with them that satisfies and fulfills you both.

You'll find a great deal of practical, useful suggestions throughout the book to assist and empower you to become a great dad in many real-life situations. This is not a book of sophisticated fathering philosophies or intriguing parenting theories. I'm more simple and practical than that. I attempt to follow Goethe's sage advice: "If a man writes a book, let him set down only what he knows. I have enough guesses of my own." I stick to sharing stories and illustrating practices that I know work. I don't pretend to have all the answers.

I do have a personal story many men will relate to and likely benefit from. And I've been researching, practicing, and teaching fathering for many years.

The first section of the book will teach you three crucial fathering skills great dads know and practice: loving your children through verbal and written **affirmation**, unending and unconditional **acceptance**, and spoken and physical **affection**. You can easily remember these as the three A's of great fathering.

The second section helps men who may not have received affirming, accepting, and affectionate fathering from their own dads to heal from those deficits so they are empowered to give to their children what they did not receive—to become the dad they wish they'd had.

The last section is all about taking action—making the lessons we've learned stick. And the epilogue is comprised of a series of additional inspiring, real-life stories written by dads just like us.

I include important and supportive statistics and quotations as endnotes for those who share my interest in such details. Otherwise, feel free to ignore the notes and just enjoy the stories and practical explanations.

> Learning to affirm, accept, and be affectionate
> with your children, and to heal if your father was
> not this way with you, will make you a great dad.

Part I

Three Crucial Fathering Skills

"We have a whole generation of men who don't understand how much they mean to their kids."

Tony Dungy, former NFL Super bowl-winning head coach

1   Why Dads Matter

As a five-year-old boy, I sat on a fire hydrant at the corner near the swim and tennis club just two blocks from our house in Sunnyvale, California, waiting for my dad's brown Oldsmobile as he drove home from work. I waited there, longing to greet my dad, wanting to be with him, to play with him, to be wrapped up in his arms, and to hear him tell me how much he loved me and how proud he was of me. I sat there for long periods on some days. My stomach ached as I wondered why he was taking so long to come home. Sometimes he didn't. On those days, I walked the two blocks back to our house feeling confused, sad, and lonely.

I stopped waiting at the fire hydrant when I was seven because my dad's brown Olds would now only appear every three or four weeks when he would come to visit Kenny, my younger brother, and me—an experience other children of divorce share with me. Dad would take us to eat dinner, to play miniature golf, or to see a movie, and then drop us off again at home—the home we used to share with him but from which he was now painfully absent. The growing sense of loneliness and sorrow became heartrending. I missed my dad. I wanted to be with him. It didn't make sense to me why he wasn't with us more.

My dad drifted in and out of my life for the next seven years until I embraced the story of Jesus as a freshman in high school. My dad was a Jewish atheist. He considered my conversion a failure on his part to properly educate and guide me. He rejected me as an idiot for believing something so stupid. He told me so. He also said I had no use for him as my father any longer since I now had God to go to. He was hurt, and in his hurt, he wounded me.

Less than two years later, when my younger brother died (I was sixteen; he was only thirteen), my dad rejected me again, telling me there was no way I could share his grief since I must believe Kenny was in heaven. He didn't know I was crushed with grief myself, did not comfort myself as he assumed, and had dismissed God from my life in my sorrow.

There were more rejections through the years. When I was in college, my dad told me he only felt guilty when we talked and therefore he never wanted to see me or speak with me again. Years of no communication passed. Then, I reached out to him, and we reestablished a minimal connection. This rejection pattern occurred two more times over the next seven years. I now recognize that though my dad was alive, I was in many ways a fatherless son. I was hungry for my father, a hunger that became a constant ache in my soul. I always felt empty inside, unloved, and unhappy. That was my experience of life.

After many years of working toward my own psychological well-being and healing, I identified my hunger as the unfulfilled longing for my father. Though I had felt a hunger in my soul for years, I began to understand that much of the longing in my life for many things I wanted but did not have was in fact a yearning for my absent father—his affirming love, acceptance, and affection. I never received these things from my dad. I wanted and needed my dad to hold me, to put his arm around me, and to tell me I was okay, that he loved me, that he was proud of me, and that he would never leave me. I ached for this.

Not clearly identifying my father hunger, I projected my need and longing onto many other things such as athletic, academic, and later professional achievements, and onto people such as coaches, teachers, and particularly women. Without knowing it, I wanted these experiences and people to make up for the lack of love I felt. I desperately sought people's approval and affirmation. I longed for physical affection. I felt unloved and unlovable from years of rejection. But that was so painful I ignored it for many years. Instead, I hoped my present accomplishments and relationships would make the pain go away.

Years of counseling and personal growth prepared me to ask for more relationship with my dad without blaming him. I was thirty-nine. My dad was sixty-seven. He visited my home for the day to play with JD, his first grandson, then two years old, and my second son, Cal, just eight months. At the end of an awkward visit, I asked my dad to be more present in our lives—in my life. He evaded my question. I pursued him. He seemed bothered by my quest—my expressed hope and expectation, my desire for more of him.

Before long, he grew agitated beyond his limit. As he shot his arms out to either side, he roared, "What do you want from me?"

I timidly responded, "I just want you to be my dad." He looked stunned and fell silent. He appeared to be thinking. My stomach tensed. My throat felt tight and dry. I hoped for something positive—some openness and warmth. I waited. I had spent a lifetime waiting for my dad—to love me, affirm me, and want me. My invitation echoed in my mind: *I just want you to be my dad.*

Finally, he spoke, "I don't want that."

He turned away from me and walked out of my house—out of my life. My hunger for him would never be satisfied. He refused to return phone messages. He wouldn't respond to pictures I sent him of the boys nor to invitations to their birthdays. Almost two silent years later, I received a phone call from his landlord informing me that my dad had been found dead in his own apartment. He was alone. His heart had failed, the report said.

> **With the last words I ever heard my father speak to me, he told me that he didn't want to be my dad.**

I still feel that loss—for my boys, for me, and for my dad. We all missed out on much I wish we could have enjoyed together. As a boy, I hungered for a relationship with my father. I never stopped longing for him. I wanted my boys to know him in a way I wish I had. I hoped my dad's experience of being a grandfather might work out better for him than being a father. None of this happened.

For reasons I neither learned nor could understand until I was an adult myself, my dad didn't want the responsibilities of any commitment, especially the responsibility of being a husband and a father. I discovered that my dad was a wounded son himself who did not seek his own healing. So my dad never actually grew up to be a man—a life task one must achieve in order to become a capable husband and father. All his adult life it was as if he was an adolescent in a grown man's body. I now understand that since the same thing happened to me.

I've spent years recovering from these experiences. Having my own children proved challenging, yet healing at the same time. Though I was a highly unlikely candidate to become a great dad, my three sons would tell you that's how they experience me now. Just writing these words makes me feel so grateful. Years ago, becoming a great dad gradually became the most important thing in my life. Knowing I'm well on my way now is so gratifying and fulfilling.

I've been teaching other men for almost ten years how to walk a similar path I have from being a wounded son to becoming a bewildered new father to being an effective and fulfilled dad. Much of that teaching first occurred in prison, of all places. I'll tell you more about that in the next chapter.

Your Father Story?

Your father story may not have as much drama or rejection as mine. I hope it doesn't. Or it may have more. The point is not to compare war stories regarding our fathers; it's to recognize that many of us didn't receive everything from our dads we wish we had. Many of our fathers experienced inadequate fathering and therefore became inadequate fathers. Some dads were abusive, violent, or severely rejecting. Most dads, however, were just not engaged the way we needed and wanted them to be. Many were busy with and tired from work, had leisure interests outside the family, or had trouble sharing their feelings. Others just didn't know, perhaps because of what they missed from their dads, how to be the kind of father many of them likely wanted to be. They may even have sworn, like many of us, that they would not be the kind of father their father was. But those vows are easily and often broken.

If you had a good father who showed his love to you not just by working hard, then count yourself fortunate. Poet, reporter, and columnist Andrew Merton wrote in his essay "Father Hunger" that "The American man who grew up with a father who was affectionate, strong, and significantly involved in the upbringing of his children is so rare he is a curiosity."[2]

If you are in this sense a rare man, be thankful. You may not need this book for your own healing, but it will help you understand what many of your friends and fellow fathers experience and need. And it will teach you how to make sure your children do not go hungry for you.

2 What I Learned in Prison About Being a Great Dad

FOR SIX YEARS, I served as a founding board member, father-hood trainer, and character formation coach for the Prison Entrepreneurship Program (PEP) in Texas. Founded by Catherine Rohr in 2004, PEP served incarcerated men who already possessed entrepreneurial passion and skills, though they exercised them illegally, and who had since demonstrated a commitment to their own transformation.

PEP established an in-prison training program to teach these men how to utilize their natural entrepreneurism and leadership in legal and ethical ways while reshaping their character and helping them reestablish their broken relationships with their families. I assisted Ms. Rohr in the founding of the program and became a trainer, entering the prison on a monthly basis to spend two six-hour days with the men—teaching, inspiring, and befriending them. What a privilege!

The most profound impact of the various topics I taught was from the teaching about affectionately affirming and accepting our children, and the experiences we shared related to healing our father wounds. Hundreds of men found healing they didn't know was possible and reestablished relationships with their children they longed to once again enjoy. Over six years, these experiences were as life changing for me as my visits apparently were for many of the men.

As part of PEP, I witnessed hundreds of men transform their lives in an environment of incredible positivity, faith, hope, education, and love. That's right—all those experiences in prison. Witness the genius of Ms. Rohr and the program she envisioned and built inside prison walls. Every executive who visited made the same essential observation: "Words can't describe the unbelievable experience of love, brotherhood, hope, and transformation I witnessed today. I thought I was coming here to give something back, but I received far more today than I gave. I've never seen love like this in the free world."

One of the inmates I had the honor of coaching for three years was known in prison as Texas Department of Criminal Justice #1318157. But I know him—and I want you to know him—as Bobby Colombo. Bobby had been imprisoned six years prior for aggravated assault with a deadly weapon while intoxicated. He regretted, more than anything, leaving his two young children without a dad when he got locked up. His daughter, Autumn, was just five years old when he was incarcerated, and his son, Alex, was only two.

When Bobby was a baby, his young, addicted birth mother gave him away to a woman who worked in a bar. She adopted Bobby and raised him without a father in a physically, emotionally, and sexually abusive home. Like millions of fatherless young men, he had no idea how to be a man or a father himself. Like many men who did not have adequate fathers, he made many mistakes and bad decisions. Bobby eventually landed himself in prison, stripped of a chance to provide for his children what he had missed—the experience of active, engaged, loving fathering. He agonized over this when I first met him. I empathized with his pain.

Bobby listened intently as I shared anecdotes about the difficult and painful relationship I had with my own father. He drank in stories about my healing journey and about my playing with, affirming, and loving my sons. Bobby wanted more. We had private conversations about his life every month I came to the prison and about his children, whom he loved but with whom he now had no relationship.

I encouraged Bobby to begin writing to his kids—to affirm them and build them up in his letters. I suggested he share how much he loved them, how much he believed in them, and how sorry he felt for not being there. After many months of writing, I asked him to promise them he would be involved in their lives as their father when released. We also talked about the importance of fulfilling promises. The disappointment of that unfulfilled promise could be as devastating for his children as his long separation. He understood that.

Bobby wrote affirming letters to his kids regularly. Slowly, both Autumn and Alex, then eleven and eight, began to communicate with him through letters. Bobby shared with me numerous letters he wrote to his children and many of the letters they wrote to him. He felt proud to bring me a letter Autumn wrote "all by herself" or a picture she drew for her daddy. Bobby had become an artist and often sent his children pictures he drew for them or cards he made himself.

It wasn't long before Autumn told her dad how much she loved him and how proud she felt of him for how he was changing. Bobby shared, through tears, "Look at this; she learned this from me. She's now encouraging and affirming me the way you taught me to do for her. I can't believe this. It's amazing."

Bobby paroled into the "free world" in March 2011. He felt better prepared and is now on the path to become the great dad he longs to be—the dad he never had. Bobby, Autumn, and Alex all counted the days to their physical reunion. But their hearts had already been reunited through letters of affirmation, love, and lots of sharing. When Autumn learned from her dad that I intended to include him in this book, she asked to write something about him.

My dad was always trying his best to make me happy. When he was in prison, he sent me letters every week and cards that he made by hand. In his letters, he always encouraged me to do my best. I got his advice and did what he told me to. I achieved a lot of things while he was serving time. My dad encouraged me to make good grades, to stay away from drugs and alcohol, and always to follow the rules. I would get so happy every time he would send me a letter. My dad made sure I got Christmas presents while he was in prison by getting into special programs that provided them for my brother and me.

I love my dad very much!

Sincerely,
Autumn Colombo

Bobby learned to demonstrate his love to his children even while still in prison through writing letters of affirmation, acceptance, and affection. In doing so, he not only rebuilt what had become non-existent relationships with both his kids but also modeled something profound that his daughter imitated—they affectionately affirmed and accepted each other. Beautiful!

Through this book, we're going to learn to do for our children what Bobby learned to do for his. Our affectionate affirmation and acceptance will build great relationships with our children—or restore broken ones—and set them up for success in every area of their lives. Most of us will face fewer obstacles to demonstrating our love than Bobby faced because of his personal background and incarceration. If he can do it, you can too.

Like Bobby, some of us may need to recover from not being affectionately affirmed and accepted by our fathers. This book is about that essential healing process as well because it's hard to give away what we do not possess—but not impossible. Where there is healing, there is freedom, fulfillment, and opportunity for lasting love and meaningful connection—for our children and also for us.

Real-Life Example

In his day, Bill Glass was an outstanding football player in the National Football League, playing on the 1964 champion Cleveland Browns and being selected to the NFL Pro Bowl four times. In 1969, Glass founded what is now called Champions for Life. It's a Christian ministry that invites professional athletes to speak to juvenile prisoners, following up with trained volunteers who commit themselves to building ongoing relationships with adolescent inmates. Glass addresses an issue that is sorely affecting the fabric of our nation: the lack of what he calls a father's blessing in the lives of young men.[3]

In an interview for the magazine *Christianity Today,* Nancy Madsen quotes Glass describing the three crucial fathering skills of affirmation, acceptance, and affection. Glass combines these skills into his phrase, "a father's blessing."

> The blessing always involves a hug and a kiss. You can't force yourself on your child, but you can hug them and get close to them physically to a certain degree without embarrassing them or turning them off. I found my kids love to be hugged and kissed. I grab my little girl by her ears and look into her eyes and say, "I love you, I bless you, I think you're absolutely terrific." That's easy with her because she's little and dainty. But I've got two boys, 280 and 290 pounds. One played pro ball, and both played college ball. They're 6'6", bench press 500 pounds, and are bigger than I am, but I grabbed that eldest son of mine recently and said, "I love you, I bless you, I think you're terrific, and I'm so glad you're mine." His shoulders began to shake and his eyes filled with tears and he said, "Dad, I really needed that." It's got to be said out loud. It's got to be stated. The blessing is also unconditional and continuous. If it's conditional, it's not love; it's a negotiation. Fathers hang with their

kids no matter what. I know a lot of fathers that disown their kids because they go to prison. But it's got to be something that is continuous and unconditional in order to be a real blessing, in order to be real love.

I wanted you to read that long quote because, in order for the story I'm about to tell you to make sense, you need to know that I shared these words from Bill Glass with the men of PEP in the Texas prison where I served. Many of the men had not seen their sons and daughters for years. Others had neglected or abandoned their children even before their incarceration.

The men of PEP were part of a very intense, approximately five-month long class. They studied entrepreneurship countless hours and endured transformative character lessons and grueling character assessments made by their class brothers and Ms. Rohr, the founder. These men were also surprisingly softened by the reflective, meditative, and tender elements she brought as a woman to the experience. She cared for the men of every class and gave of herself to them in profound and meaningful ways, including giving every man in every class what she called a "sweet name" that served numerous softening and bonding purposes.

These were names like "Buttercup" or "Baby Cakes" or "Angel." No kidding. Somehow Ms. Rohr created a profound sense of safety that made it okay for tough men to not only allow for the use of sweet names but to enthusiastically embrace them and proudly identify themselves by them. They addressed one another by their sweet names and even introduced themselves this way to the executive volunteers who came in to teach or to visit for special events such as Selling Night or Etiquette Night, or to serve as volunteer judges for the business plan competition at the end of each class.

Many inmates would quit the program along the way or were removed for lack of character, unwillingness to change, or the breaking of the strict PEP rules. But for the men who made it through to the end, they would be honored by a real graduation ceremony—in prison!

For the graduation of Class III, Ms. Rohr asked David Harmon, the class valedictorian, to give a speech at graduation. This graduation felt particularly special for us at PEP because it was the first time the Texas Department of Criminal Justice allowed children to attend. For the prior two classes, they had made an exception by allowing parents to come to the graduation service, but this time, they made a unique, unprecedented concession and allowed the children of the men to be present as well. All of us, but especially the dads in the class, were bubbling with excitement as well as some palpable apprehension.

When David stood up and made his way to the platform, wearing what for him—and for many of the other men—was his very first cap and gown, the first time he had ever graduated from anything in his life, he stood at the microphone and tried to compose himself. Then, he looked out at the crowd. He saw his PEP brothers sitting closest to the stage. Behind them, we sat, the PEP staff and invited executives. And behind us sat the families. This proud, honored PEP graduate set his gaze to the back of the audience and said, "My dear wife and my thirteen-year-old daughter are here today. I haven't seen my daughter in too many years."

With his voice beginning to crack a bit and tears beginning to form in hundreds of eyes, he continued, "I'd like my wife and daughter to stand up, please, so you can see them." They did, and we clapped. I could feel embarrassment overtake his daughter. She appeared to want to hide somewhere as she covered her blushing face. Then he looked right at her and said, "Baby, I am your father. And you are my daughter. And I just need you to know that I love you, I bless you, I think you're terrific, and I'm so glad you're mine."

All of us were sobbing, as was his daughter. Then David smiled through his own tears and added, "I learned that in here."

Marvelous! In that stunning moment, frozen in my memory and heart forever, I grasped the importance of teaching fathers how to love and affirm their children. I realized that day that my life somehow needed to move in a direction of sharing with more men the value and power of loving our kids through these three crucial fathering skills—affirmation, acceptance, and affection. I dedicated the second half of my life to inspiring and empowering men everywhere to become greater dads. This book and the founding of The Great Dads Project represent the beginnings of my answer to that call.

3 Three Secrets to Dad Success

O VER MANY YEARS, I've read a great deal about child developmental needs as well as various fathering practices. What children
appear to need to know and feel most from their fathers and what
fathers are eminently capable of communicating can be encapsulated
in three core practices or crucial fathering skills I call affirmation,
acceptance, and affection: the three A's of great fathering.

Affirmation refers to verbal and written words of specific praise
regarding our children's character, decision-making, and treatment
of others more than their appearance, achievement, or performance.
To affirm means to declare something to be true. So when you affirm
your children, you declare what is true *about* them and *for* them. You
declare what is true about their character and their potential. Your
words, that is, your verbal or written expression of your high view of
them, then become the basis of their self-awareness and identity. Your
regular affirmation can actually neutralize the negative messages the
media and their peer group may be speaking to them. So affirmation
means stating our belief about what is true in and about our children
and encouraging what we hope to be true as they grow. Affirmation is
about creating the reality we envision in our children's character and

for their favorable future through our belief in them and our praise of them. Our affirmation helps our children believe they are smart, capable, and able to achieve whatever they set their good minds to.

Acceptance speaks to our unconditional and unending embrace of our children no matter what they do, how they fail, what they choose to value or believe or pursue, or with whom they associate. Yes, that includes their choices of friends, music, clothes, boyfriends or girlfriends, and later even their marriage partners. Yes, that means accepting them even if their beliefs or values differ from ours or if they choose different political affiliations or, even, sexual practices—you name it. Unconditional and unending acceptance means accepting our children no matter what, even if we disagree with or disapprove of something they do, say, believe, or practice. It's a tricky distinction—one many dads fail to make to our own detriment and certainly to our children's. Our unconditional and unending acceptance communicates to our children that they belong. It helps them know and feel that they are ours, we want them, and we will never, ever turn them away.

Affection applies to both spoken and physical expressions of love, tenderness, warmth, and care. Affection may be demonstrated a bit differently for boys and girls, at times, particularly as they mature. Regardless, a dad's physical and spoken affection is critical to the healthy development of children, particularly their sexuality—their understanding of themselves as young men and women as they reach puberty. A father's affection helps children know they are loved and lovable, as well as worthy of good, healthy, fulfilling relationships in the future.

Why are affirmation, acceptance, and affection such powerful experiences between a father and his children—or in some cases, between a father figure and a younger man or woman who never received these from his or her own dad? Because affirmation, acceptance, and affection go to the core of character formation and the establishment of healthy self-esteem. These three crucial fathering skills give to a child a gift that will last their lifetime. These three fathering practices define what it means practically for a dad to love his children. Here's how you can express your love powerfully and meaningfully.

When children miss these experiences from a loving father, they suffer a wounding that can be deep and long lasting. This wound cries out for healing—a healing that can be experienced when a father or father figure is present and the wounded son or daughter seeks to heal and grow.

Real-Life Example

One of my father mentors, Cory Ishida, senior and founding pastor of Evergreen Baptist Church in San Gabriel Valley, California, stunned me with his father-like love when I was a younger man. I believe I was about twenty-nine. He stood in for my father who wasn't capable of extending his affirmation, acceptance, or affection to me. Even when I became aware enough as an adult to know I missed and longed for my dad's love and felt healed enough to ask him for it without blaming, my dad wasn't able to give it.

But Cory did. One evening, he placed his hands on my shoulders, looked me in the eye, and spoke to me as a father would his own son. He spoke regarding specific character traits he saw in my life such as the way I expressed compassion for people and gave of myself as I taught and coached high school students at the time. He affirmed me and prayed for me. He told me how proud he felt of me and that he believed I would become successful in whatever I set my mind to accomplish because of the good he saw in me.

For me, receiving Cory's affirmation felt like such a powerful, painful, and healing experience. I say it felt painful because I still wished it had been my own father speaking words such as these to me. Yet hearing loving affirmations from an older man whom I admired proved to be powerfully healing.

The Word "Blessing"

Like Bill Glass, Cory referred to this as a father's blessing. The word "blessing" conjures up for many people religious connotations. The word often is used in religious settings and practices but is not necessarily a religious word.

Dads, blessing our children can be—but does not need to be—a religious experience or rooted in a particular faith tradition: Jewish, Christian, or otherwise. Fathers of all religious faiths or of no particular faith commitment can—and ought to—bless their children.

What children need to know and feel is that their dad is proud of them, accepts and affirms them, loves them, and pictures a bright and beautiful future for them. They need to know they are wanted, valued, and belong. For this reason, I use quotations in this book from authors who sometimes, though not often, refer to a father's blessing. Whenever you see the word "blessing," know it is just shorthand for a great dad affirming his children, demonstrating acceptance of them, and sharing affection.

Putting It into Practice

When my boys were babies and toddlers, I developed an intentional practice of communicating my love, particularly when I said good night to them. I've practiced this all their lives. I sit on each son's bed with the lights out, place my strong hand on his chest, head, or face, and I first speak to him words of love and affirmation. I tell my son how glad I am to be his dad and what a special boy he is, specifically naming something I see in him, enjoy about him, or of which I'm proud. I speak words that communicate my full and never-ending acceptance of him. And I always hug and kiss him before I leave his room, usually on his cheek or forehead but sometimes on his mouth or even on his back when I've been giving him a short massage—anything to show physical affection to my son.

For many years, I borrowed some words I found in the New Testament to formulate an affirmation I often used. There is a moment at the baptism of Jesus when God, represented as a Father, speaks to Jesus publicly, so everyone there can hear. I borrowed God's words and a few others from another part of the New Testament, added a few of my own, and made up my own affirmation I regularly spoke to each of my boys at bedtime.

These are the words each of my boys has heard thousands of times: "You are my beloved son [I use his name here], in whom I am so well pleased. I will never leave you nor forsake you, for you are my son, and I'll love you forever, no matter what." Short, simple, and to the point, yet full of rich, affirming, committed love. I always touch my boys in a warm, affectionate way when I speak like this to them.

Verbal and written affirmation, unconditional and unending acceptance, and spoken and physical affection communicate a life-shaping message to our children. We'll take a thorough and practical look at each of these three crucial fathering skills one at a time in the three chapters that follow.

4 Why Saying "I'm Proud of You" Makes All the Difference

Affirmation: an assertion that something exists or is true

COUNTRY MUSIC LEGEND Reba McEntire sings a heartrending song titled "The Greatest Man I Never Knew." The song expresses the broken heart of many girls whose fathers never told them they loved them. The reality is that we influence our children, well into their adult life, by what we communicate—sometimes by what we fail to communicate. Our words, spoken and written, shape the way our kids see themselves and therefore what they believe they can achieve and the relationships they believe they deserve—the same way our fathers' words shaped us and what we believe about ourselves.

Dads, we need to tell our daughters and sons:
- ▸ How great we think they are.
- ▸ How proud we are of them.
- ▸ How great we think it is to be their dad.

- ▸ How we wouldn't want any other kids in the world besides them.
- ▸ How lucky we think we are to have the kids we do.
- ▸ How much we love them.

> It is not enough to *love* them; we need to *tell* them—the more the better. If we don't, our silence could be and often is misinterpreted.

We may think our kids know we love them because of all we do for them, all we sacrifice, and how hard we work. They need more than that. They need to *hear* it in order to *feel* it. Telling our kids we love them is vital, but it's even more helpful to tell them why. The more specific our affirmation is, the deeper and longer lasting its impact.

My friend, Bill, has three children—a four-year-old son, a two-year-old daughter, and an infant baby girl. I shared with him how meaningful it is to our children when we give our affirmation consistently and specifically. He said, "I understand the importance of verbal words of support and affirmation and the distinction between insightful and specific words of affirmation and an empty and reflexive 'I love you.' I got a lot of the latter from my mom growing up. I appreciated it, but it wasn't very helpful to shape a positive self-identity." Our kids certainly need to hear that we love them and think they're great. It's even more powerful when we tell them specifically why.

Real-Life Example

Nancy is a forty-five-year-old wonderful mother of two. She has also enjoyed a very successful business career and has now founded her own enterprise, including becoming an author of four books (see www.zelawelakids.com). She is fortunate to have a loving, supportive father. When she was fourteen years old, her father affirmed her in a way that had a profound impact on her and the direction of her life. He said, "You are so intelligent and wise beyond your years."

She told me, "I felt loved and knew from that day forward my father respected me and thought my ideas were valuable." She added, "I never worried about talking with my dad after that or sharing my thoughts because he esteemed my ideas and opinions and wanted to hear what I had to say."

That father's vital and well-timed verbal affirmation set a course for Nancy's adult life. Though he had been a constant source of loving support and regularly affirmed Nancy, she now recalls, "This particular comment stuck out and made me feel so respected and mature." Because of her dad's belief in her, she came to believe in herself—that she had what it took to be successful in the world and that she would make a valuable contribution to it. And she certainly has and continues to. What a gift Nancy's father gave her in his verbal affirmation.

Tell Your Kids You Love Them—and Why

Our children need our affirmation—to hear that we love them and are proud of them and why. It hardly matters *how* we say it or write it. What matters is that we do.

Suzanne Braun Levine writes in her book *Father Courage: What Happens When Men Put Family First*, "Children, we are told over and over again, know when they are loved; there is no wrong way to love them—except, perhaps, not to go the extra mile of delivering the message."[4]

Most dads already know this on one level, and we believe it. Our problem, if one exists, is not a lack of knowledge, but a lack of modeling. Perhaps our dads weren't great at communicating their love and affirmation to us with words. So even though we want to, we're not sure how to do it ourselves. It may not feel natural to us.

Real-Life Example

When JD, my oldest son, turned four years old, I took him to a San Francisco Giants baseball game. He had just begun to like baseball, and I taught him to catch and throw in our driveway. He also had a growing fascination with trains. We lived within a long walk of the Diridon train station in San José, and the train stopped at the north end of the line just blocks from the Giants' stadium in San Francisco. It was a perfect setup.

For JD's birthday, we rode the train all the way to the city together and walked hand in hand to the ballpark, carrying our gloves so we could catch that elusive foul ball. I purchased matching Giants T-shirts and hats for us to wear. We ate all the snacks we brought with us in our blue canvas backpack while we watched the game. It was a beautiful, sunny day, and the stadium was packed.

On the way home, we played catch on the train in our seats that faced each other on the second level. We talked about the game the whole way home as JD imitated the pitcher and the batters. Lots of people on the train smiled at me, nodding their heads in enjoyment of us, and many commented how happy JD seemed, and how lucky I was. What a great day—seven hours of trains, baseball, conversation, and affection. I must have told JD twenty-five times how much I loved him, how much I loved being his dad, and how much fun I had all alone with him. By this time, his two younger brothers had been born, and we were busy.

A couple weeks later, I repaired a dripping sink in our master bathroom. I needed new O-rings. I once heard that taking one of your kids along when you run out on errands is an easy way to spend some one-on-one time together. This time, I took JD. I strapped him into his booster seat in the back of Mom's champagne-colored Durango, and off we went to the Orchard Supply Hardware near our house.

We were about a mile from the house when I happened to look in the rear view mirror. I noticed JD wore his Giants T-shirt and hat that day. I had read somewhere that verbally reinforcing memories was a good thing to do with young children, a way of revisiting the experience to keep it alive in your child's mind. This seemed like a perfect opportunity to try it.

"Hey, Buddy, I see you have your Giants T-shirt and baseball cap on."

"Right, Dad."

"Who gave those to you?" I asked, pretending not to know.

"You did, Dad."

"I sure did. I love getting things for you and being with you, Son."

"I love being with you too, Dad."

"Do you know why I bought those for you?"

I expected him to say, "For my birthday getaway." Then I'd talk some about how great it was. Instead he shot back, "Because you love me *sooooo* much."

I felt astonished. I thought, *He's only four years old, and he already knows the reason I buy him things and enjoy being with him is that I love him so much. Amazing.*

I had somehow been able, through regular and consistent verbal affirmations, in just four years, to implant that knowing and that secure knowledge in my son's soul. He *knows* and *feels* his daddy loves him.

I wish I had known that about my father at JD's age. As we drove to the hardware store, I still missed that confidence. I felt sad about the hole in my heart, the not knowing I've lived with all my life and the sense that my dad didn't love me. At the same time, I felt happy and fulfilled about the security my verbal affirmations had produced in my son. I realized I had given him a gift that would last his lifetime. That realization inspired me to make sure I did this same thing for my two younger sons as well.

"My daddy loves me." There's nothing more important for a young boy or girl to know and feel.

Real-Life Example

I once read about a dad who wrote letters to his children and how meaningful it was to them. I tried it. I wrote to each one of my boys and sent those letters in the mail on staggered days—not email, but real, old-fashioned, it's-gonna-cost-me-a-stamp mail. I enjoyed how surprised they each were to get mail from me. My oldest, JD, decided to save his to read at bedtime as I sat with him on his bed. When he finished, he set it down, looked right at me, smiled, and spoke only one word: "Nice."

Two days later, when Cal, my middle son, received his, he also read it at bedtime. Then he and Kai, my youngest, climbed into their bunk beds. When I came into their room to say good night to them, Kai asked Cal from the lower bunk, "What did *your* letter say?"

"You want me to try to repeat a hundred words?" responded Cal.

"No, just tell me what it said."

"Well, it basically just said how much he likes me."

Kai asked me, "Dad, am I going to get one of those letters too?"

"Well, you just might," I said with a knowing smile. His face lit up.

His anticipation made my small effort worthwhile. He was happy knowing his letter would arrive soon. He ran to the mailbox the next two days until he found his treasure.

Here's one of the letters I sent. I include this just to give you an example of the kind of thing you might write to your kids. Create your own. But do write something to each of your kids this week. Try it.

Hello my wonderful Cal,

I wanted to send you this special note to tell you how very much I love you and how I am thinking about you all through my day, even when we are not together.

I love being your dad. Being a great dad to my three sons is one of the most important parts of my life. I wouldn't trade being your dad for anything.

I'm very proud of you, of the way you are working hard in your schoolwork and in soccer. I fully enjoyed watching you enjoy the World Cup this summer. You love it so much. I know that if you dedicate yourself to it and work as hard as you can, you can achieve your dream of becoming a professional soccer player. I would love to come to your pro games, just the way I love to watch you play now, even though your team stinks. You amaze me and impress all who watch you. You never give up, and your skills are getting better and better all the time. You are a great athlete and a coach's dream because of your good character, attitude, and work ethic.

I also love working out with you at the HIT [High Intensity Training] center. I hope we can do that for many years together. It's always better for me when you and your brothers are with me. I'm already looking forward to our getaway for your next birthday. I love spending one-on-one time with you.

Well, my son, I wrote this letter to you because I love you. You are a gift to me. And I'll love you forever, no matter what!

Real-Life Example

The soccer team Cal played for that year was not very good—they lost almost every game. They played one particular summer game in scorching heat, and their opponents slaughtered them. Part way through the first half, our goalie went out of the game with heat exhaustion. The coach moved Cal from midfield to goalie. With our goalie out and Cal out of midfield, our defense looked like a sieve attempting to hold water. The other team must have taken thirty shots on Cal in the second half alone. They scored ten goals against us in that game, about half of those against Cal. Often two or three of their players attacked without a defender to slow them. A dad from the other team, not knowing I was Cal's dad, commented on the outstanding play of our goalie. He admired Cal's near-solo effort. I thanked him.

When the game ended, I saw Cal shake hands with the other team's players and the referees and then walk across the field by himself. His head was down, his eyes staring at the ground. I could see tears in his eyes.

I ran out to the middle of the field, knelt down, wrapped both my arms around him, and said, "Cal, you did not fail today. You were amazing in goal. You must have stopped twenty-five shots. You just had no help back there on defense, and you played a talented team."

I moved Cal only slightly from me, put my hands on his shoulders, looked into his eyes, and continued, "I know you're discouraged, but I'm as proud as ever of you. You played your heart out, as you always do, but one man does not make a team. One of the dads from the other team commented on how great a player you are and what an outstanding effort you gave today. Hold your head up, my son. You gave it all you could today; you brought all your talents. And that's all anyone can ever ask of you. Even if it didn't achieve the outcome you wanted and even though your team lost, you are a winner, my son. And I'm immensely proud of you."

As I spoke my verbal affirmations, I saw Cal's head and eyes lift. His shoulders rolled back into place. He seemed to stand a bit taller. Somehow, my words—and my physical embrace—soothed my son's sorrow, breathed life into his saddened heart, and helped him weather that storm. I felt thankful to be there for that moment and that I knew to take advantage of it.

Written Affirmations Work Wonders

Here's another written affirmation I adapted. I typed it and printed it on a full sheet of paper in a big, bold font like you see below. Then I taped it to the wall right next to each of my boys' beds, right near their pillows. When I came into their rooms that night to tuck them in, they asked me about it, and I read it out loud to them before I hugged and kissed them good night.

No matter what you do, no matter where you go, no matter how long it's been, no matter what it costs:

> As long as I have a penny, you'll never be broke.
> As long as I have food, you'll never go hungry.
> As long as I have a coat, you'll never be cold.
> As long as I have an arm, you'll always be hugged.

And if I don't have a penny or food or a coat, or if my tired arms are too old to hug anymore, then come and stand by my bedside and hold my hand and know that as long as my heart beats in my body, your daddy will always love you!

Two days later, it surprised me when I went into Cal and Kai's room at bedtime to discover they had both memorized this. Then they recited it to me. The note apparently meant as much to them as it did to me—perhaps even more.

On another occasion, I typed out and left appreciation notes for my boys on the breakfast table. When they awoke and came to eat, they found this affirming note waiting for them:

Mom and Dad work hard to provide the money needed to house, feed, clothe, and provide recreation, vacations, and sports opportunities for our family. We do this because we love you and value our family time so much.

> We appreciate the contributions you each make toward the family's well-being and happiness by doing the household tasks we ask of you. That really helps to make things manageable.
>
> Thank you for all you do.

Written notes don't have to be formal like these or long. Short notes left on a white board or a Post-it note at the breakfast table or a note placed in a lunch bag, even affirming words sent by email or text, can communicate some of the love we want our kids to feel.

More Verbal Affirmations

Sometimes I'll say to my boys for no apparent reason at any random time, like driving in the car, "Hey, you know what?"

They'll now often say, "Yeah, you love us."

"What? How did you know I was going to say that?" I ask in feigned surprise.

"Because you've told us about a gazillion times," they say.

Perfect! Just what I intended. Verbal and written affirmations make a meaningful and lasting impact.

Real-Life Examples

Jerry Hall is one of my closest friends and a great dad. (You'll read his story in the epilogue.) Whenever Jerry departs for a business trip, just before he leaves the house, while his family is still sleeping, he writes and leaves short love notes for his fourteen-year-old daughter, his twelve-year-old son, and his wife. He says they now expect this whenever he's traveling.

I have other friends who make good use of technology and send texts or emails in the middle of the day just to remind their kids they're thinking of them and to tell them they love them. Other dads Skype with their kids when they're traveling. If you don't live with your kids for whatever reason, Skyping, emailing, texting, and writing regular notes of affirmation to them is crucial to maintaining contact, fostering a loving relationship, and shaping your kids' character.

> Whatever you can do to be with your children
> and to speak and write verbal affirmations
> to them will deepen your relationship
> and show your kids you love them.

Affirmation Starters

Dads, here are some effective affirmation starters that I use with my boys. Try using each of these in the next two weeks with each of your kids. You can speak, write, text, or email these. Use them. Watch how your words fill your children's hearts as if blowing up a big balloon. When I first began using these affirmation starters, I wrote them on an index card and kept them in my truck to help me remember them and to remind me to use them.

- ▸ One thing I admire most about you is . . .
- ▸ One of my favorite memories with you is . . .
- ▸ One of the funniest things you have ever done is . . .
- ▸ One of my proudest memories I have of you is . . .
- ▸ I like it when you . . .

Real-Life Example

A friend of mine sent me the following email about the affirming words he regularly heard from his own father:

> You are completely accurate about affirming and encouraging words. My dad is a master at that. I really think he was able to hone his skills as a coach and as a shop

teacher before he was a dad. Before I was born he taught and coached for eight years. I've never talked to him about this, but my guess is that during that time, he was able to experiment with what really worked with his students and athletes. And then he just used that with me, and my sister. He was a great dad who made us feel loved.

Make It Stick!

- ▸ We show our kids how much we love them when we speak and write our affirmations.
- ▸ Our affirmations help our children believe they are smart, capable, and able to achieve whatever they set their good minds to.
- ▸ Dads powerfully nurture children through regular verbal and written affirmations.
- ▸ When we affirm our kids, we build them up by our words and give them a lifelong gift of loving belief and support.

Why "I Love You No Matter What" Means So Much to Your Kids

Acceptance: a favorable reception; an act of believing;
nonjudgmental love; opposite of rejection

M Y DAD DID SOME THINGS really well. One of the great things he imparted to me—a gift I have passed on to my own children—was a respect for all people, no matter what their culture, language, or skin color. I learned from my dad to overcome prejudice. My dad and I cheered on the Civil Rights movement together when I was in grade school. I felt close to my dad in those days and believed he was proud of me for the way I embraced his acceptance of all people. My boys have my dad to thank for that heritage.

My dad also taught me to respect my body—not to abuse it with alcohol, drugs, or tobacco. I'm grateful to my dad for those values he modeled for me and passed to me in our early conversations.

For a good portion of my young childhood, my dad also built in me a sense of security and belonging. Because of words my dad spoke to me, I believed there was nothing I could do that would turn his love away from me. He told me so, repeatedly. I actually remember my dad telling me when I was in middle school: "Keitho [his favorite nickname for me], I will always love you. You can tell me anything anytime. No matter what you do, even if you were locked up in prison or turned out to be gay, you would always be my son, and I would always love and accept you."

I later learned that being incarcerated or gay were the worst things my dad could imagine. That was his way of saying if I hit bottom, he'd be there to love me and help me up. I felt loved and secure in his acceptance and devotion. I knew I belonged with and felt valued by my dad.

Imagine the shock I felt the day I returned home from tennis camp as a freshman in high school and announced to my Jewish yet atheistic father I had embraced the teachings of Jesus at camp and invited Jesus into my heart. He was stunned and angry. He challenged my new, tenuous beliefs and belittled me. He actually wondered aloud, "How could any son of mine be so stupid as to believe such ridiculous things?"

Many years later I'd learn that my dad felt he had lost me as his son that day and that he was jealous of what he believed to be my redirected affection toward and loyalty to God. Soon after, as I mentioned in the first chapter, my dad told me: "You don't need me anymore; you can just go to God now." He was hurt, and in his hurt, he distanced himself from me and wounded me. Our relationship deteriorated over the next several years. When my brother died, my dad fully rejected me.

A few years later my dad said, "I only feel guilty when we communicate. I don't ever want to see you or talk to you again." That security of belonging, of being loved and valued I felt as a child, had been fracturing for years. Now, it was shattered.

Many years later, after I had reestablished some limited communication with my father, I asked him about this. I reminded him about his expression of never-ending love and devotion even if I were incarcerated or gay. "What happened?" I asked. "Why did my choosing to follow Jesus break the love we had?" My dad told me: "That was the one thing I never imagined happening and the only thing I could not accept."

I still don't know why his atheism was more important to him than I was or why my alternate choice of life-stance was so devastating for us, but my father never got over it, and we never reconnected with the love we shared when I was young. It took me a long, long time to recover and heal from that rejection and the many that followed in the ensuing years. (I'll share more of that journey in the second section of this book, "Healing a Father Wound.")

As a child, I needed the same assurance every little boy or girl needs—to believe that I was loved for who I was and that would never change. I needed to know that my parents loved me not because I was smart or handsome or a good athlete or a great student. I needed to believe that even if I couldn't speak properly or run fast or ride a bike well or paint a pretty picture or play the piano, those shortcomings would never change how much my parents loved me, wanted me, and accepted me. I needed the assurance that my parents' love for me was not based on anything I had to achieve or accomplish and that their love would never fail, never be taken away, and never diminish.

When little boys or girls really know this, that assurance builds a strong and secure foundation for believing we belong—that we are loved and lovable the way we are without having to earn our parents' affection. Those secure beliefs about ourselves and about our parents point us in the direction of good and healthy relationships in the future.

It is the lack of knowing these critical, security-producing feelings that leads to so much of the loneliness, feelings of being lost with no place to belong, and the desperate search so many young people find themselves in for acceptance.

Many children given up for adoption often find themselves later struggling with such feelings, believing their birth mother didn't want them, even in those cases where that wasn't true.

Plants grow best when they are provided the proper environment to flourish—the right amount of soil nutrients, water, and sunlight. It's also true of people, especially children. We give our kids the gift of a lifetime when we provide a guilt-free environment in which to mature; when they don't fear rejection because of failure, shortcomings, or mistakes; when they are allowed to think for themselves and become their own persons, not little replicas of Mom or Dad; when they are not forced to dress, or wear their hair, the way we want them to; and when they are not pushed to choose the beliefs and values we hold. We allow them to flourish like a well-nurtured plant.

Our unconditional and unending acceptance of our children provides security, belonging, and marvelous nurturing for their growth as human beings into responsible and strong adults who have their own voice and feel good about who they are. What a gift!

> Our unconditional and unending acceptance communicates to our children that they belong forever, no matter what. They are ours, we want them, and we will never, ever turn them away.

This is the second crucial fathering skill. Easier said than done in some cases. The fine and difficult distinction is to know the difference between unconditional and unending acceptance on the one hand and blind, undiscerning approval with no boundaries on the other—and to stick to that key distinction diligently or to come back to it when we fail. We can disapprove of something our children do, say, or believe, even provide discipline while still completely accepting them. And that is what they ultimately *need* to know, though they, of course, *hope* for both.

> Approval is nice; acceptance is essential and should never fail.

Make It Stick!

▸ Children need the assurance that their parents' love for them is not based on anything they have to achieve or accomplish and that their parents' love will never fail, never be taken away, and never diminish.

▸ When little boys or girls really know this, that assurance builds a strong and secure foundation for believing they belong—that they are loved and lovable the way they are without having to earn their parents' affection.

▸ Those secure beliefs about themselves and about their parents point them in the direction of good and healthy relationships in the future.

▸ Remember that completely accepting our children for who they are and what they choose for their own life does not mean approving of all their values or choices. That is a key distinction too many dads miss, or lose along the way. We can strongly disagree with and disapprove of something our child does, says, thinks, or chooses while still communicating how much we love and accept them. That's hard to do, but so important.

▸ If you are struggling with something you disapprove of in your child, try this helpful exercise. Write down exactly what it is you don't like and cannot accept. For instance, "I hate that my teenage son is so lazy and disrespectful." Or, "I can't stand the friends my daughter chooses." Or, "It drives me crazy when my kid cries so long and throws such temper tantrums." Write down whatever it is that really bugs you. Then next to each line write something such as, ". . .but I completely accept you, my son." Or, ". . .but I accept you, my daughter, forever, no matter what." Do that each day for ten days in a row and see if this helps you with the essential distinction between disapproval of a behavior or choice and acceptance of the person.

6 A Hug Is Not "Just a Hug" When It Comes from Dad

Affection: a type of love; fondness; tender attachment

WE COMMUNICATE OUR LOVE when we touch and hold our kids, and when we speak tenderly to them in ways that say or mean "I love you." The father pictured in Reba McEntire's song "The Greatest Man I Never Knew" never spoke to or touched his daughter in an affectionate way. The result was that she never knew he loved her. How was she to know?

Spoken and physical affection is not just something daughters require; sons also crave a dad's affectionate touch. Boys tend to need more sustained physical contact with their fathers, often shown through activities such as sports and through play, even roughhousing, while girls seem to require more tender, physical affection.[5]

Author Neil Chethik surveyed 300 men and interviewed in-depth another seventy, all of whom had lost their fathers to death. In his book *FatherLoss: How Sons of All Ages Come to Terms with the Death of Their Dads*, he shares a potent statement about sons who did

47

not get affection from their fathers. Many women report the same effect. Chethik writes: "When a son doesn't get affection, in any form, from his father, the resulting wound can be deep and lasting. Second only to the abuser in generating resentment among the sons I interviewed was the faraway father, the distant dad, the patriarch who was unavailable or uninvolved. Whether the father meant it or not, the message to the son was clear: You don't matter."[6]

So many of the inmates I spoke with shared that they never felt love from their fathers. When I asked them about physical affection, they disclosed they'd never been touched in a loving way by their dads. Some of them broke down in tears. Many admitted feeling worthless, believed they would never amount to much, and had become convinced they didn't matter. Their lives fulfilled those tragic beliefs.

One short, muscular man with a barrel chest approached me after I spoke one evening. He looked into my eyes for a moment without saying a word. I noticed his eyes fill with tears. He wrapped both his arms around me and buried his head against my chest. I held him as his entire body began to shake with sobs of anguish. Through his tears he revealed his father never touched him except to beat him with a belt: "My daddy never held me or touched me with tenderness." He composed himself enough to say, "When I was six years old, I saw my father shot to death." He burst into heaving sobs again as I held him. He mumbled, "The man who shot my dad was his father—my dad's dad."

He cried for a long time as I embraced him. I thought, *How does a man recover from this? How does this kind of experience shape a child's idea of what a father is and what it means to be loved by your dad? How will this man learn to love his own children and to express that love through physical affection?*

And yet, in that moment, I also realized that here I was, a big, older man, a father-figure, holding this tough, hurting son. I was showing him physical affection as I accepted him, listened to his story, held his pain, and affirmed him with my words. Without intentionally creating the situation, I observed how healing this must have been for him. What an honor to stand in the place of an absent father to affectionately affirm this wounded son.

Why Father Nurture Is as Important as Mother Nurture

I can only imagine what comes to mind when you read the term *nurture*. I first pictured a nursing mom with a hungry infant at her breast. One thing was clear: that wasn't me. I once sat on the couch, holding JD, my first son, as a one-week-old infant while my wife got some much-needed rest. I stared at him, loving him and feeling happy about this big transition in my life—becoming a dad. I cradled him in my arms so his head was to one side of my body, his feet to the other, holding him about chest-high, as if holding a football.

The strangest thing happened; he tried to suckle. He wanted to nurse—on me! I felt awkward, a bit embarrassed, and inadequate. There was no way I could meet his need. I relived that experience when I first saw the title of Dr. Kyle Pruett's first book, *The Nurturing Father*. What could he mean?

Kyle Pruett, M.D., Professor of Child Psychiatry at the Yale School of Medicine, Yale University Child Study Center, is a pioneering researcher who conducted the country's only long-term study of the impact on children of primary caretaking fathers. Today we call them stay-at-home dads. Pruett's findings not only establish that dads, all dads, not just stay-at-home dads, *can* nurture our children but also that it's good for us to do so and it's invaluable to our children.[7] Dr. Pruett believes dads provide things for children through nurturing that even the best mother-nurturers can never supply because they're moms and we're dads; moms and dads nurture differently.

Pruett affirms that father nurture is a tender, warm, loving experience, but it's also a masculine one, not to be patterned after the way a mother nurtures children. To *nurture* a child means to take care of a young one and to encourage the child to flourish. It does not imply method. As dads, we have a nurturing style all our own, and it's as important for our children's growth and development as our wives' style. More than that, it changes *us*. When we nurture our children, we grow too. We take steps toward becoming the great dads we long to be.

"The great man is he who does
not lose his child's heart."
— Mencius, fourth-century B.C.E. Chinese philosopher

Showing Affection Isn't Easy for Some Dads

I empathize with men who find showing affection difficult. It's something I had to learn to do with my own children. Dr. Pruett suggests cultural forces have reinforced the stereotype that only women nurture while men hunt. In our culture, hunting equates to working and making money. Pruett writes, "One of the most tenacious obstacles to a man's discovery and sponsorship of his own nurturing capacities is the early and often reinforced lesson that the economic security of his family is his most sacred, possibly only, legitimate domain. Men learn early that the 'correct' way to father is *indirectly*: loving by fostering, securing, protecting, guiding, sponsoring—not necessarily by touching or holding."[8]

Is this where we want to be? We can overcome the mistake of indirect fathering by affirming our children with our verbal and written words, by accepting them in an unconditional and never-ending way, and by showing them love through our spoken and physical affection.

In *The Blessing*, authors John Trent and Gary Smalley warn parents that "neglecting to meaningfully touch [your] children starves them of genuine acceptance."[9] This needs to change. Our children need and want us to touch them in warm, affectionate, and age-appropriate ways. We can share physical affection in tender moments of touching, holding, massaging, or appropriately kissing, particularly with daughters. But we can and often should show affection by playing, wrestling, roughhousing, and fist or chest bumping too, particularly with sons.

> Physical touch and play communicate acceptance, belonging, and value to a son. Dads communicate these important messages to a daughter more often through warm, affectionate, and nurturing touch.

Children Need to Feel Their Father's Love

Sons and daughters need more than *knowing* that their dads love them; they need to *feel* loved by their dads. There can be a big difference. A physical touch helps our kids experience the love we have for them in our hearts. In his book *Back to the Family*, clinical psychologist, author, speaker, and radio host Ray Guarendi writes of how his father *showed* his love.

> Affection is now and always has been openly displayed in my family. My father is one of the most masculine men I know, but he always kissed my brothers and me, and he would tell us verbally how much he loved us. A lot of the boys I grew up with had fathers who were extremely uncomfortable in expressing affection to them. I suppose they were afraid it was not a manly thing to do. I do not doubt that their fathers loved them; it is just they were the kind of men who only knew how to say "I love you" by getting up and going to work every day so they could provide the things their families needed.[10]

How do you show your love? Spoken and physical affection is essential for kids to feel the love we have for them.

Bill Glass spoke of his father: "My earliest recollections are that my father would sit on my bedside and rub my back and tell me what a fine boy I was, and almost every night, he would kiss me on the mouth. He was a pro baseball player, a very manly man. But he had no problem expressing his love and blessing to me and to my brother and sister."[11]

I do that with my boys every night I'm home and often during the day as well. I'll be honest; it's something I had to learn to do because my dad wasn't around to do this with me. It felt awkward, at first, to kiss my boys. But I understood its importance. I determined to push through my awkwardness so my boys could *feel* how much I love them. I'm a big guy. I'm 6'2" tall and weigh 205 pounds. When I hug, kiss, and roughhouse with my boys, they feel it.

Real-Life Example

At bedtime one night, when my youngest son, Kai, was nine years old, he read to me from one of his *Boxcar Children* books. Then I turned out his light and hugged and snuggled him. He said, "Dad, you have no idea how great it is having a great dad like you." He reached out and grabbed me around the neck and pulled me close.

"Kai, thank you. You have no idea how nice that is to hear and how happy it makes me. Being a great dad to you and your brothers is one of the most important things in my life. You're right that I don't know how great it is to have a great dad."

"You didn't even have a dad," he said.

Just to be clear, I responded, "Well, Kai, I did have a dad, but he wasn't around much, and we didn't get to spend the kind of time together that you and I do. And we didn't snuggle the way we do either."

"Yea, that's what I meant."

We hugged again. I kissed him and said good night. My heart felt full. I'm grateful I've been able to build the kind of relationship with my boys that didn't last with my dad for me. I've made lots of mistakes along the way, more than I wish to recount. But I've done at least this right: I love my boys with words of affirmation and affection. And I show them I love them by the way I touch, hold, and kiss them. That love has covered hundreds of failures.

Through verbal and written affirmations, by unconditional and unending acceptance, and through spoken and physical affection, we become great dads who build (or restore) loving relationships with our kids.

Dads and Teenage Sons

JD is fifteen now. I've been affectionate with him since that magical night he emerged from the womb and I held him for hours as he cooed in my arms for the first time. Since then, I've built a strong habit of holding, snuggling, kissing, and touching him, as I have with each of my boys. But JD is a young man now. In fact, he's a couple of inches taller than his mother. His voice has changed and he is growing hair everywhere. I love it. Developmentally, he needs me more now than ever.

A teenage son needs his father's affirmation of him as a young man. JD studies me to see what being a man looks like. I can feel it. When we're together, some thick unseen substance—the mystical stuff of manhood poet Robert Bly called "brown ooze"—passes from my body to his. I feel needed and valuable.[12]

Although JD and I still remarkably enjoy a great deal of hugging, back scratching, hand holding, and an occasional kiss on the cheek or forehead, he also needs a different kind of physical affection now. He's experimenting with his own developing masculinity. That gets worked out for us in physical contact that's a bit rougher. He wants to challenge me in sports, wrestle with me, and punch me all the time.[13]

We developed this routine when we go to brush our teeth before bed. He says, "Come here, I've got something to tell you." As I approach, he starts to punch me in the chest, throw me on the bed, pin me down, and punch me some more. Of course, these are play punches and they—mostly—don't hurt. He loves this. He laughs the entire time. He wants and needs to conquer Dad to establish his own manliness. Being bigger and stronger than JD won't last much longer, so while I still can, I return the affection by reversing positions, pinning him, punching him, though never hurting him—on purpose—while he laughs until he gives. Then we stand up and hug, just to begin the routine over again. Sometimes we even get our teeth brushed.

My younger sons are heading in this direction. They ask me to show them the physical games I used to play in high school such as a hand smacking game that requires quickness and toughness and a balance game that demands physical strength and clever strategy. They want to be physical with me in competitive ways. They want to best Dad. And I want them to.

Dads, our teenage sons' need to conquer us shouldn't challenge our egos. The struggle shapes our sons for their future. They need to beat us, in time. I'm raising my boys to do so. If I let them best me too soon, they'll sense it, and that won't fulfill their need. If I refuse and fight them, unwilling to pass the mantle of champion, the eventual and inevitable victory will come at too great a price for both of us. So I'm in some mysterious way the foe to be conquered, but at the same time the mentor and coach who encourages them to surpass me.[14]

In the midst of this man stuff, I never stop hugging, kissing, holding, and snuggling my boys. They still sit on my lap or get wrapped up in my arms when we watch sports or movies together, even JD, my young teenager. They often ask me to scratch their backs or rub their calves and legs. I oblige with a smile, hoping these moments of shared affection never become a thing of the past.

JD has recently initiated a bedtime routine with me where he asks me to do my "special stuff." He's referring to me using lotion to rub his sore calves from all his athletic practices, and then to rub his back and shoulders before he goes to sleep. I'm glad to do this every night I'm with him because I never know how long this will last—his wanting me to touch him this way. His desire for my touch might dissipate any time. For now, I'm happy he still wants my touch, and I'm more than willing to serve him this way. It's a subtle way to be physically affectionate with him every day.

Many teenage boys begin to feel embarrassed about a father's affection—at least they say they do. That's normal, especially in public. Don't take it personally or feel rejected, Dad. Our sons still need sustained contact from us. If they don't want to be hugged, then pat them on the back. Punch them affectionately in the arm. Fist bump and high five them the way I do every day with my middle son, Cal. He initiates high fives with me all day. Wrestle with them. Figure out ways to touch your teenage son that feel okay for him. He still needs your physical affection. And your touch communicates your love for him. He needs to feel you touching him.

Dads and Teenage Daughters

As daughters reach puberty, they look to their fathers to help them define their femininity. They want to know whether their fathers accept them and find them valuable and attractive. Physical affection with teenage daughters will look different from all the man-play. But the goals and effects are quite similar.

Friends with daughters tell me they stroke their hair or brush or braid it for them. They massage their backs or legs after sporting events. They hold hands. They sit on their beds at night and touch and kiss them, usually on the forehead or cheek, in tender, appropriate ways as they talk about their day, their dreams, or the boys they like. Wrestling and tickling demonstrate physical affection with daughters, though as they age, less of this seems age-appropriate.

A daughter's puberty means big changes emotionally and physically. Suddenly, daddy's little girl is growing up and becoming a woman. She's growing breasts. Many men feel a natural and normal attraction to their daughters in this challenging period of life. However, for most men, that doesn't feel natural. Many men are scared by their feelings, as if the attraction itself were somehow incestuous. It's not; psychologists tell us a father's attraction to his daughter, and hers to him, are entirely normal and age appropriate.[15]

What is not appropriate is acting out that attraction in sexual ways. And sometimes it's tricky to draw a clear line between normal and appropriate affection and a more sexual touch. Because of this, some dads withdraw all affection during this crucial period of a daughter's development of her femininity. When fathers withdraw and withhold affection for fear of sexual feelings or actions, many daughters misinterpret Dad's retreat as rejection. It can be a wounding experience that damages a girl's image of herself as attractive.

Countless studies suggest that girls who have sex experiences as teenagers are often looking for physical affection they did not get from their dads.[16] Dads, we go a long way in loving and protecting our daughters by sharing the physical affection they long for, deserve, and need from us, even into their teenage years and beyond. Don't withdraw. Do whatever work you need to do to become comfortable with your own sexuality, even the normal feelings of being attracted to your daughter. Don't act on those feelings but acknowledge they are there and natural. Talk about this with your wife, if you're married, or with a trusted female friend or counselor if you are not. You are not alone. Your daughter needs your approval more than ever during the teen stage of her development into her womanhood. Your ongoing, age-appropriate physical affection will communicate great love and approval.[17]

Be a great dad today. Tell your kids how much you love them, and touch them in a way that makes that message stick.

Make It Stick!

▸ To ***nurture*** a child means to take care of a young one and to encourage the child to flourish. It does not imply method. As dads, we have a nurturing style all our own, and it's as important for our children's growth and development as their mother's style. More than that, it changes *us*. When we nurture our children, we grow too. We take steps toward becoming the great dads we long to be.

▸ Boys need sustained touch from their dads through their teen years. Figure out ways to touch your son in a way that feels right and okay for him. And do so regularly.

▸ Girls need to know their father approves of them and finds them attractive. Your tender, age-appropriate physical affection will communicate this to her. Touch her in appropriate and loving ways. Don't withdraw when she hits puberty because you find her attractive. Talk about that with your wife or another trusted female friend or counselor.

▸ Our spoken and physical affection means the world to our kids. It helps them feel valued and loved. Tell your kids today how much you love them and why. Show them by some form of physical affection.

7 Building Your Child's Self-Esteem

G REAT DADS WHO have learned to give affirmation, demonstrate acceptance, and show affection build within their children a secure foundation for their future. These crucial fathering skills shape who children become because they substantially determine what kids believe about themselves, what they imagine they deserve by way of personal friendships and intimate relationships, and what they think they can or cannot accomplish in the world.

Henry Ford affirmed the reality that what people believe about themselves determines what they accomplish. He said, "Whether you think you can or you can't, either way, you're probably right." I've had all three of my boys memorize Ford's quote. The point is that a father's affirmation, acceptance, and affection help his children believe they *can*. When we believe in them, they tend to believe in themselves. We thereby help them to achieve whatever they set their minds to.

A father's affirmation, acceptance, and affection allow a child to grow into a man or woman who can move out into the world away from the childhood that established his or her self-respect, self-control, self-discipline, and self-confidence. The three A's give our children the gift of a strong and secure sense of self.

When daughters or sons have received their father's affirmation, acceptance, and affection, they're able to grow to maturity and wholeness, move out into the world, and establish intimate relationships that are substantially free of the multiple issues and problems that many young people today seem to carry into their marriages—issues from a childhood deprived of their father's love that have not been resolved or healed.

Many young men and women are still longing for and in search of their father's affirmation, acceptance, and affection. That search often continues within their marriages. Men and women try—usually subconsciously—to get from their partner what they never received at home. Some distance themselves in fear of further rejection or because they don't know how to be close or because intimacy feels unfamiliar. As I did for so long, many are *repeating without remembering* their loss from the past, often sabotaging relationships and situations to match their internal sense of shame, loss, and sadness—much of which may result from a deprivation of a father's affirmation, acceptance, and affection. (I'll explain and illustrate *repeating without remembering* from my own life in the second section of this book, "Healing a Father Wound").

Dads, by lovingly practicing the three A's, we give our kids the gift of freedom to engage in and enjoy the most important relationships they'll ever have—their marriage and their own children. We set them up for relational success. We build into them a great sense of themselves and fill them with love and confidence so they have tremendous internal resources from which to give of themselves to others.[18]

Through affirmation, acceptance, and affection, a dad says, "You belong here. I accept you the way you are. You are immeasurably and irreplaceably special to me. I want you. I value you. I love you. I'm proud of you. And I believe in you and what you will make of your life."

Fathers Can Paint a Picture of a Bright Future

In his book *Making Peace with Your Father*, psychologist David Stoop speaks to the power a dad has to imagine for his children a special future. He says, "The [father], then, is ultimately the source of 'blessing' on his child, and the blessing is rooted in the father's acceptance of his child. What does this mean in more concrete terms? One thing it means is that the father helps draw his children into the future. He helps them dream. These are not the dreams of night, but of a Don Quixote: dreams of overcoming obstacles, of meeting challenges, of making a genuine difference in the world."[19]

By pointing your children toward the future like this, you build within them the confidence that it is bright for them and that they are fully capable of achieving what they desire.

> We build them up. Our belief in them
> inspires their belief in themselves.

The Power of a Father's Affirmation, Acceptance, and Affection

Christian writer Donald Miller precisely sums up the immense power a father has to positively shape the life of the children he loves and believes in. In *To Own a Dragon: Reflections on Growing Up Without a Father*, Miller expresses the emptiness within himself, a consequence, he deems, of his own dad abandoning him. He speculates: "I wondered if people who grow up with great fathers don't walk around with a subconscious sense they are wanted on this planet, that they belong, and the world needs them."[20]

A few pages later, Miller notes: "Dwight Eisenhower said his mother and father made an assumption that set the course of his life—that the world could be fixed of its problems if every child understood the necessity of their existence. Eisenhower's parents assumed if their children weren't alive, their family couldn't function."[21]

Former Vice President Al Gore, speaking at The National Fatherhood Initiative's Third Annual National Summit On Fatherhood in Washington, D.C., affirmed the shaping power of his father's affirmation and presence in his life. He said: "Don't ever doubt the impact that fathers have on children. Children with strongly committed fathers learn about trust early on. They learn about trust with their hearts. They learn they're wanted, that they have value, and that they can afford to be secure and confident and set their sights high. They get the encouragement they need to keep going through the rough spots in life. Boys learn from their fathers how to be fathers. I learned all those things from my own father, and I count my blessings."[22]

> Mere words fail to capture the immense and transforming power of a father's affirmation, acceptance, and affection or the distressing wound when these crucial fathering elements are withheld. It's like trying to describe the beautiful experience of intimate love or the destructive power of a tornado.

David Stoop says, "Unfortunately, the blessing is often conspicuous primarily by its absence. We often know we are missing something, even when we do not know what that 'something' is."[23] This is the emptiness Donald Miller articulates. It's an experience readily identified by millions of us who grew up without fathers or who had dads who didn't know how to affectionately affirm us.

Some dads just weren't around or engaged enough to positively shape us. *New York Times* columnist Bob Herbert concludes: "Kids who grow up without a father never experience that special sense of security and the enhanced feeling of belonging that comes from having a father in the home. So they seek it elsewhere. They don't get that sweet feeling of triumph that comes from a father's approval, or the warmth of the old man's hug, or the wisdom to be drawn from his discipline."[24]

Bill Hybels is the founding pastor of one of the largest churches in the United States. He describes his grief over his father's death: "Several years ago my father, still a relatively young man and extremely active, died of a heart attack. As I drove to my mother's house in Michigan, I wondered how I would continue to function without the person who believed in me more than anyone else ever has or will."[25] I marveled at what it might be like to know that your dad believes in you like that. *What might that do for a young man's or young woman's sense of self and what he or she might accomplish in life?*

That's the power of a father's affirmation, acceptance, and affection. These three crucial fathering skills shape a child for life. They build self-respect, self-esteem, a deep confidence, and a belief within your children that they are smart, talented, and capable of doing anything they set their good minds to accomplish. What a gift when the three A's are given. Yet what a hole it leaves in a child's soul when they are withheld or absent.

In his book *Champions for Life: The Power of a Father's Blessing*, Bill Glass writes of the way his strong father routinely affirmed him when he was a boy. When Bill turned twelve, his dad contracted Hodgkin's disease. Over the next two years, Bill watched his dad wither and eventually die. He writes, "It began to dawn on me even in my teens that a father's blessing has an almost mystical power. When he was there, 'all was right with the world.' I needed my dad to help establish my identity. For years, I floated, not knowing who or what I was—my dad was not there to tell me. I couldn't figure it out. I was in a haze. This is a common problem."[26]

Indeed, all too common. Yet it's a problem we dads can begin to eliminate as we learn to affectionately affirm and accept our daughters and sons. How do we do it? How can we capture this mystical power and awesome privilege and give the tremendous gift of these three crucial elements of our love to our children? The following chapters provide practical suggestions and inspiring stories.

8 How to Turn Daily Life into Extraordinary Moments

A JEWISH PROVERB SAYS, "Do not withhold good from those to whom it is due, when it is in your power to do so."[27] The very next verse urges us further. Only slightly revised to fit our context, it says, "Do not say to your son or daughter, 'Go, and come back, and tomorrow I will give it,' when you have it with you."

Dads, don't withhold your praise and affirmation from your kids—it's in your power to give it. Lay your praise on thick, but be real about how you do it. If it becomes a joke or part of teasing, it loses its impact in a hury.

> Be sincere, be affirming, be positive,
> and praise *whatever* you see your kids
> doing right *whenever* you observe it.

Numerous times a day is a reasonable goal. You don't need to wait for a special occasion. Take advantage of day-to-day opportunities to affirm your kids. Say it out loud, and say it often.

> Kids need far more praise than they
> do correction or criticism.

Affirm Character

There doesn't need to be a big event going on in order to affirm your kids. Just catch them doing something right anytime. Then praise them. Be careful not to just affirm their behavior, accomplishments, achievements, or appearance. Make sure to also and often praise and affirm their character, since that's what matters most and will last the longest.

> Our children's character will ultimately shape
> all their experiences and relationships.

Whether or not one of my boys gets an A in math is not nearly as important as seeing him become an honest and responsible person. Whether or not your daughter is physically graceful or beautiful is not as important as the development of her mind, personality, and character. Praise character; affirm choices that show honesty, wisdom, discernment, compassion, generosity, and unselfishness. When you do that regularly, praise for performance or appearance finds its natural place too but will not mean everything to your kids.

> Our children begin to put things in order,
> to know that who they are matters more
> than what they do or how they look.

Why praise character? Attorney Michael J. Smith dedicates part of his practice to the Home School Legal Defense Association. In that capacity, he provides both legal and parenting counsel. Smith says, "We should focus on praising our children for character development. When words of praise are only linked to a child's performance, they lose much of their impact. Children who have to perform to get a blessing retain a nagging uncertainty about whether they are ever really good enough. They ask in their heart, 'Am I loved for who I am, or only for what I do?'"[28]

Celebrate performance, but praise character, good decision-making, wise choices, acts of service and compassion, responsible behavior, and truth telling.

Affirmation, Acceptance, and Affection at Bedtime

An experience that happens nearly daily in my home is bedtime—we try to make our boys go to bed every night. Not too long ago, they initiated something they call The Midnight Poker Club (much thanks to my mom for introducing poker to them). We've discovered that on some late nights, all three boys pack into one of their closets, turn on the light, and play poker until the wee hours of the morning. Busted!

But before they get up to play, we think we're putting them to bed for the night. When we do, I want that experience to be a good one for my sons—I want my boys to feel positive about the last interaction of the day with me.

I sit on each one of their beds, one at a time, or sometimes I lie down with them, touch them in some meaningful, affectionate way, and affirm them. I want them to know and *feel* that I love them and am immensely proud of them. I do this even if things didn't go well that day or if for some reason I had to discipline them. I never want a distant or strained feeling between us to be the last one they have for the day. So I affirm them affectionately every night I'm with them at bedtime.

It's good for them, and it's good for me. It draws us close by reminding both of us how important our relationship is and what I really think of and feel for them, even if in the moment those feelings are buried somewhere and I have to go find them. It still astounds me how meaningful this is for my boys. They love it and ask for it if for some reason I forget or feel too tired. They want this time with me. And I gladly give it.

Real-Life Example

One summer evening last year, Cal and Kai were outside playing. I went out and stood nearby as I watched Cal training Kai as a soccer goalkeeper, and I smiled. My heart felt full as I heard Cal not only instructing Kai but also repeatedly saying things like, "Good job, Kai. That's right. That's the best throw you've made yet. Great." I stood there and thought, *That's the kind of thing Cal has heard consistently from me, and he's now repeating what he's experienced—affirming his little brother.* I felt fulfilled as I enjoyed my sons and recognized how important my modeling is for my boys. They watch me and listen to me. They want to be like me, so they imitate what I say and do.

Later that evening, as I said good night to Cal, I cupped his face in my hands and said, "Son, I want to tell you how delighted I was to see you training Kai tonight. You're such a good big brother and a good coach. I loved hearing you praise and affirm him and build him up."

Cal smiled, then reached out and grabbed me to hug me. He didn't say a word; he just wanted to be as close physically as we could be. That's how my affirmation affected him. When we affirm with our spoken words of love and pride, our children often want to be closer to us.

It was seemingly a small thing, a regular event on a regular day, my boys playing soccer outside in our yard, but I took advantage of that simple event and turned it into a special opportunity to affirm my son with affection. You can do the same kind of thing.

> We teach our kids how to affirm
> others by modeling it ourselves.

For Dads Who Find This Difficult

Michael J. Smith gives practical advice to dads who may not find it easy to give praise and affirmation. He writes:

> If praising your children (or anyone for that matter) doesn't come naturally to you, you can try an old sales trick to remind you. Place ten pennies in one of your front pants pockets. Every time you praise your kids, transfer one penny to the other pocket. The goal, of course, is to transfer all ten pennies every day. One family came up with a great, creative idea to praise, affirm, and encourage their kids. They created a "Celebrating Our Family" news and bulletin board and put it where everyone could see it. Mom and Dad would then post their kids' successes, achievements, and displays of good character up so everyone in the family could see them and celebrate them.[29]

The point is that there does not need to be a big event happening for you to affirm your children. Simply take advantage of the regular, day-to-day experiences of life while you look for the character, positive qualities, and actions your children manifest. Then speak your words of praise, love, respect, and pride.

9 Cashing in on Special Life Moments: Why the Little Things Count

SOME OF THE HIGH SCHOOLS in our area allow eighth graders to try out for some of their junior varsity teams if they need players. JD decided he wanted to try out for the Bluegrass United soccer team. That summer, I took him to his first open session workout. When we drove up, JD's eyes grew large. He was very quiet and sank back into his seat a bit. He didn't jump out of the truck as I had expected. Every kid on the field was big—at least four inches taller than JD, and heavier. They were all high school boys; it was a bit intimidating.

JD and I sat in my truck and talked about it. We then went and introduced ourselves to Zac, the head coach. Zac welcomed JD and sent him out to warm up with the big boys. I stayed and watched the entire practice. JD's play and effort amazed me. He did just fine playing with the team.

When it was over, I met JD at the edge of the field. I wanted to take advantage of this special moment—he didn't let his fear paralyze him. I greeted him with a fist bump, put both my hands on his shoulders, looked into his eyes, and said, "JD, I think that's the best I've ever seen you play. And I know that's the hardest I've ever seen you work. I'm proud of you for overcoming your fear and giving it your best. You were very fun to watch."

He just smiled and said, "Thanks, Dad." He seemed happy the rest of the night. He appeared proud of himself. He was more talkative than usual, and he kept smiling. He somehow grew up in front of our eyes that evening. I marked the day with that short, simple, but meaningful affirmation at the field.

In his bestselling book, *A Million Miles in a Thousand Years*, Donald Miller shares a touching story about a dad making the most of a special moment for his daughter, a moment he almost let slip by.[30] I love how this dad made a great recovery and ultimately communicated his affirmation, acceptance, and affection. Miller writes:

> My friend Randy recently created a great memory with his daughter. When his daughter entered high school, she started to get more interested in girl things, and the two of them didn't talk as much as they used to. When she got asked to the prom, she was very excited. Her dad simply responded by saying congratulations. She quickly slid past him and jumped up and down in front of her mom. He didn't mean to be dismissive, but he didn't know what he was supposed to do.
>
> About a week later he was watching *SportsCenter* when his wife and daughter came home with a dress. They didn't say anything to him, knowing he wouldn't be interested, and went back to the daughter's bedroom so she could put it on. When she came into the living room to show her dad, he turned down the volume and told her she looked nice, that it was a nice color, but when she curtsied and thanked him and walked away, he knew he should have said more.

He wanted to tell her that she was beautiful and that she was his princess and all the stuff fathers find so hard to say to their daughters. He turned the television back on and tried to pay attention to the scores, but all of this kept bugging him. Then he came up with an idea. He decided to create a memorable scene, if you will. He turned off the television and went into his closet and put on his suit. Without letting his wife or daughter see him, he found the family camera and knocked on her door. When his daughter opened the door, she was still in the dress and her mother was sitting on the bed with stick-pins in her mouth. My friend said his wife almost swallowed the pins.

"Honey," my friend said to his wife, "would you mind taking a picture of us?"

"Daddy, you're wearing a suit," his daughter said, confused.

"I want to look good in the picture too," he told her.

The three of them ended up dancing in the living room until one in the morning, my friend and his wife telling stories about their own prom dates and how they wish they would have known each other in high school.

Beautiful. Nice recovery. Here's a great dad making the most of a special moment—giving his love mostly nonverbally. He acted it out. Sometimes we can give our affirmation, acceptance, and affection even without many words.

Real-Life Example

My middle son, Cal, participated in the Soccer Olympic Development Program (ODP) for the first time two years ago when he was eleven.

Part of that wonderful experience included an invitation to attend a regional training camp during the summer, including players from ODP teams from ten other states. This four-day camp took place in DeKalb, Illinois, just west of Chicago, about a seven-hour drive from where we currently live in Kentucky.

When we first heard about the camp, Cal felt a bit nervous. He had never spent a night away from both Mom and Dad. The young players would stay in college dorm rooms with other players their age, train all day, every day, and play games in the evening. At one of the winter training sessions, we were told privately by one of the coaches that parents would be allowed to attend the evening games. This seemed comforting to Cal.

We turned the camp into a fun adventure we would have as father and son. We would drive to the camp and enjoy all that travel time together. I would stay in a hotel near the college and use my days alone to work on this book. I'd come to every game in the evenings and video his matches—his idea. We would drive home together when it ended. Cal would stay in the dorm with the players and be mostly on his own, but at least we would have nightly contact, and that settled him.

We spoke often about this and had fun thinking about and planning the trip. At the last winter training session, however, the head of ODP in Kentucky made it abundantly clear that *no parents*—except designated chaperones—were allowed on the college campus, at all, at any time, during the entire regional camp experience. He was also clear that the kids were expected to ride the bus provided from Kentucky to and from the camp.

I felt very disappointed. I think Cal felt afraid. He announced he no longer wanted to go. He's not one to readily embrace new and big adventures, and this one I think felt beyond him.

Now what? Plan B. This one would take some creative parenting. Debbie, Cal's mom, and I went to work. Both of us talked positively with Cal for a few weeks about all the potential benefits of this experience: the friends he'd make, the opportunity to improve his game, the great coaching, and the quality of players he'd face. We talked about how much he had grown up, how capable he is, and how confident we felt that this would be a good experience for him. We talked about ways he could feel good about the trip, such as bringing some good books for the bus ride and bringing a cell phone so he could call home whenever he needed or wanted to.

After several weeks of this kind of positivity and affirmation, his thoughts began to shift, and his attitude changed. He decided he would go and that he would have a good experience. I felt so proud of him.

I drove Cal to the bus at 4:30 AM the day he departed. There in the parking lot, in the dark, before he boarded, I stood in front of him, put my hands on his shoulders, looked into his eyes, and spoke the affirmation I had planned for weeks and memorized: "Cal, this is going to be the best soccer experience you've ever had. You're such a capable and confident young man. I completely believe in you and support you. You'll make some good friends on this trip and have so much fun. I can't wait to hear the stories. Bring all your talents, Son. Give everything you have to this experience. Hold nothing back. You'll remember this the rest of your life. Go with my immense pride in you and my love filling you. I love you, Buddy. There's no one like you. Have a great, great trip. And call whenever you want to."

We hugged each other. And I gave him a wrapped soccer book called *A Beautiful Game: The World's Greatest Players and How Soccer Changed Their Lives* as a gift for the experience. Inside the front cover, I had written out the affirmation I spoke to him so he would have it with him the entire trip. I told him to open the gift on the bus. Then he got onboard and started his adventure that turned out to be everything he hoped for.

I thought about and planned that early morning send-off for a long time prior to the day it happened. I crafted the affirmation I wanted to speak. I bought, wrote in, and wrapped the book ahead of time. It was a special moment for both of us, marked by a simple gift and a father's loving affirmation.

Look for Special Moments

Look for special moments in your experience with your children. It might be a dance, music recital, horse show, or sporting event. It could be an activity like white-water rafting, skydiving, bungee jumping, or perhaps something less adventurous such as fishing, hunting, going on a dinner date, visiting a museum, or watching a sunset together. It might be a child showing some aptitude for painting, singing, skating, dancing, or playing a musical instrument. It could be a birthday party or a service project or a theater production. When a special moment occurs, make the most of it by creating and sharing a special, spontaneous or crafted affirmation with your child.

> Your affirmation makes the moment even more special than it already is and reminds your children how special they are. That's a reminder they need far more often than we might realize. And your affirmation makes it stick.

10 Celebrating Life's Milestones with Your Child

IN THIS CHAPTER, we're going to consider how to honor special rites of passage our children experience by adding our affirmation, acceptance, and affection. Rites of passage are the significant transitional events or milestone experiences in a child's life when time is marked by moving from one developmental phase of life to another such as beginning to walk, learning to ride a bike without training wheels, or starting puberty.

A rite of passage might be signaled by a significant event such as a teenager getting a driver's license or landing a first job. It might be graduating from high school, going away to college, or moving out of the family home for the first time. Other rites of passage could include getting married or possibly divorced, becoming a parent, or even experiencing the loss of a child. Not all rites of passage are necessarily positive experiences, at least not initially, but they are moments that change our lives forever.

> Rites of passage signal moving from
> one stage of life into another.

At these important transitions in life, a father's affirmation, acceptance, and affection can add meaningful and powerful stability and create lifelong, positive memories. Author Neil Chethik reports: "One man I interviewed, a business executive, said he had received a traditional Mexican blessing—a *bendición*—from his father when the son left Texas at age nineteen to look for work in California. The blessing, uttered by his father in Spanish, affirmed that the son was ready for the journey ahead and called upon God and humankind to look after him. It also softened the son's feelings toward a father who had often been harsh and uncompromising."[31]

I'll share some examples of rites of passage to pay particular attention to—and to encourage your creativity.

The Onset of Adolescence

Is there a more turbulent time in the life of a child than the massive hormonal and physical changes going on in a teenager's body and brain during adolescence? This is often a destabilizing and, for some, scary time of transition if not attended to by a parent or some other loving, strong, supportive adult figure.

David Stoop notes: "The beginning of adolescence is an especially critical period for both sons and daughters. Adolescence is the time of forging an identity, and the father plays a crucial role in helping both his sons and his daughters define who they will be as adults. Central to this process is the development of sexual identity: being comfortable with what it means to be a man or woman."[32]

An Adolescent Becomes an Adult

Stoop acknowledges how critical this rite of passage *out* of adolescence is and how timely a father's affirmation can be at this transition. He writes that an "important task of fatherhood happens at the other end of adolescence—when the father introduces his child to the world as an adult in his or her own right, when he imparts his 'blessing.' Something special happens when a father can sit down toward the end of the adolescent stage and discuss with his son or daughter—adult to adult—the tasks and choices that lie ahead. When he does this, he leads them into the real world, away from the shelter of mother and father."[33]

A father's affirmation, acceptance, and affection are crucial at this momentous rite of passage. Stoop elaborates regarding this important life transition. "Adolescence must come to an end. We all know men and women who seem to be trying to remain eternal adolescents. They simply have never grown up. They go through life acting like irresponsible, fun-loving, thrill-seeking kids. Invariably, these are people who have never experienced a definite closure to adolescence. Both [sons and daughters] need some form of the father's blessing to mark the end of childhood and the arrival of adulthood."[34]

This is true of so many men. It was true of me for many years. Without a father to call us up into manhood, we get older on the outside but remain adolescents on the inside. It is nearly impossible to intimately love a woman and wisely and warmly raise children when we still feel like boys ourselves. Lacking our father's affirmation, acceptance, and affection, many of us don't know how to grow up to be men and act like men. So we keep searching for the elusive affection and the missing affirmation that we are good enough, brave enough, smart enough, and capable enough.

Stoop writes, "Many of us are still looking for that father's blessing. Not surprisingly, we are looking for it in the logical place: our fathers. One man told me that all he wanted in life was for his father to put his arm around him and say, 'Son, you're doing great.' Sadly, his father died before he was able to talk to him about what he needed and wanted. The man felt lost, as if he were somehow unable to graduate from the awkwardness of adolescence into confident manhood."[35]

Even when I was thirty years old, I still felt like a teenager starving for my father's affirmation, acceptance, and affection. No wonder I still didn't feel like a grown man. I had never been released into—or even prepared for—manhood. A dad provides the gateway for a son to become a man and for a girl to become a woman—to feel like a man or a woman in a grown-up's world.

A Girl Becomes a Woman

A dad plays an exceptionally important role for his daughter. Dads model for sons what it means to be a man. For daughters, we teach them through our example what to expect from men and how to relate to them. Our affirmation, acceptance, and affection call our daughters into womanhood and encourage them to embrace their own special feminine mystique and power.

Tom Pinkson is a clinical psychologist and father to two daughters. He wrote an intriguing and beautiful essay called "Honoring a Daughter's Emergence into Womanhood." Pinkson detested the cultural messages about and some of the degrading sayings related to a young woman's menstrual cycle. As his two daughters were approaching this rite of passage, he talked to them about it ahead of time and asked them to let him know when it started for them because he wanted to celebrate it with them by taking a camping trip together and giving them a special gift.

Pinkson regarded his daughters' first menstrual cycle as a wonderful sign of emerging womanhood and designed a special ceremony and celebration to honor his girls at this important transition. He writes, "I was distressed by the disrespectful messages and treatment that girls and women receive in our society. I wanted my daughters to be honored, to be blessed for who and what they were, young women just coming into their power and responsibility for creating their lives."[36]

This great dad took his girls camping, one at a time, when they started their cycle. They stayed up late at the campfire and talked about becoming a woman. Pinkson gave each of his daughters a special gift that symbolized their womb becoming a fertile place that could create life (for the oldest daughter, it was a gourd). This dad replaced the cultural negative messages with positive affirmations and made this rite of passage for his girls something special to remember. It became his way of honoring them in their transition to womanhood.

A father's affirmation, acceptance, and affection for his daughter are crucial throughout her life. Dr. Evelyn Bassoff, psychologist and author of *Cherishing Our Daughters: How Parents Can Raise Girls to Become Strong and Loving Women*, writes, "If our daughters are to flower, they need optimal conditions. Almost always this means being lovingly cared for by mother and father. It is from her mother that a girl learns to be a woman; it is from her father that she learns what to expect from men in the way of love and respect."[37]

In her article "Leaving the Vulnerable Open to Abuse," Gracie Hsu takes this further, highlighting the impact of a father who does not affirm his daughter's growing femininity: "Today with the rise in illegitimacy and divorce, fewer fathers are around to protect and defend their daughter's safety and honor. With more girls lacking the love and attention that only a father can give, more of them are willing to settle for perverse alternatives, namely, seeking intimacy with predatory adult men."[38]

Dads, let's affirm, accept, and show affection to our daughters throughout their entire lives. But let's pay special attention to this important rite of passage when our little girls become women.

A Real Life Example

A friend named Beth remembers how her father affirmed her before she left for college. He honored this rite of passage by creating a beautiful experience and writing a meaningful letter. Years later, Beth recalls the evening this way.

The summer before I left home for college, I felt so grown up and eager to embrace my independence and meet the world.

A few weeks before I was to leave, my dad—with whom I had always been close—invited me on a special date. He'd made reservations at the fanciest restaurant in town, The Plumed Horse, known for its white linens, crystal, elegant décor, and amazing cuisine.

We both got all dressed up. I wore a nice skirt and blouse and high-heeled pumps. Dad donned his best suit and tie. I can still picture the table for two where we sat and dined. Our wonderful meal ended with a thrilling splurge, flaming cherries jubilee! Decades later, I don't recall what I ordered for dinner, but I vividly remember—now with tears—how special I felt. My dad wanted to spend time with me and demonstrated how much he cherished me.

That evening, he presented me with a letter he'd written: "Thoughts for My Daughter on Departing for College (an open letter)." In those two typed pages, full of fatherly love and wisdom, he shared his hopes for me as I embarked on a life away from him, my mom, and our family. There were four points, simple but profound:

1. Grow, expand, and learn.
2. Make choices that are life giving.
3. Question but don't abandon your faith.
4. Remember that just as you are God's child, you will always be our child and will always have our love.

He expanded on each point, sharing from his heart, admitting his own failings, and punctuating with biblical truths.

At the time, I knew his words—and the time he'd invested writing them—demonstrated his immense love for me. But they didn't fully sink in. I was so excited to start the next phase of my life—to leave the nest, to try out my wings, to discover my own truths—that I read through the letter quickly and the words somewhat bounced off me.

But I saved that letter. Today, I realize that my father's words—both in his letter and in other meaningful talks we'd had through the years—influenced my life. This priceless letter now reminds me of our dinner date when he made clear how valuable I was. Because my dad invited me out, spent one-on-one time with me, and made it so special and memorable, I felt how important I was to him. By taking me to the fanciest restaurant in town, he made clear I was worth splurging on. By writing that letter, he gave me a tangible reminder of his love and hopes for me.

I was seventeen that evening and took many things for granted. Today, as a grown woman, I know the gift I received, having a dad who was—and still is—present and interested in me, who affirmed me, made me believe I could be and do anything I set my mind to, and who, at an important rite of passage, invited me out on a special date I'll never forget. I wish all children had a father like mine.

The Father of the Bride

I performed a beautiful marriage ceremony years ago. Before the bride and groom shared their vows, the bride's father read an exquisite letter to the couple. He had kept it a surprise—his daughter had no idea he was planning to do this, though he had secretly arranged it with me. This great dad praised his daughter publicly for the character she had developed and the strong, loving, independent, and responsible young woman she had become. He praised her choices of friends, of vocation, and of a husband. He welcomed his new son-in-law and spoke to him of how happy he was to give his daughter to his loving care. Then he looked into his daughter's eyes and said, "Honey, I'm so happy to be your dad, and I'm so proud of the remarkable and beautiful woman you have become. I give you away today with tremendous joy and pride. You will have my blessing forever."

There wasn't a dry eye in the place as he read his letter of affirmation, acceptance, and affection and spoke of his love, joy, and pride. This great dad treated his daughter's wedding day as a rite of passage. He gave her away, in the most profound sense of those words, and affirmed her and her husband publicly. Not a bad way to start such a significant relationship.

You can make a profound impact on the most important relationship your son or daughter will ever forge by giving a thoughtful and well-planned affirmation at their wedding ceremony, or at some appropriate moment near that special day.

A Boy Becomes a Man

David Stoop notes, "Many anthropologists believe that the formal initiatory rites into manhood in some of the more primitive cultures are a direct result of the universality of this conflict at the beginning of adolescent development."[39] These initiatory rites welcome young men in particular into their manhood and declare publicly, upon completion, that the boys have become men. Though the rites have changed today in our culture, our boys' need for such an initiation has not.

Christ in the Rockies (CITR) is a Christian-based organization in Colorado.[40] They have designed an outdoor experience for dads and their adolescent sons to honor this rite of passage. The program encourages bonding and helps dads extend a special affirmation in a meaningful way at a crucial time of life—their sons becoming men.

My friend, Jon Lachelt, is a board member of this nonprofit organization. He's also their rock-climbing instructor. Though Jon has four daughters, he is well aware of the need for dads to affirm their sons at this critical life transition. I asked Jon to describe the experience. He wrote the following:

> CITR grew out of a desire to provide a Christian rite-of-passage event for young men that is more than just a ceremony. To that end, CITR created a four-day adventure in the Rocky Mountains for fathers and sons to discover together what it means to become a man. Every element of the week is focused on building and, if necessary, restoring the relationship between a father and son. Each day the men participate together in high-adventure activities such as mountain biking, rock climbing, and in the evenings exploring God's perspective on manhood. Over the course of the week, each father gives a public blessing to his son, affirming his love and commitment to his son, expressing what he is proud of his son for, and sharing the good qualities and abilities he sees in his son. The week culminates in a moving rite-of-passage ceremony where the father invites his son into the company of men and issues a personal charge, calling his son up to live out the high calling of manhood.

This calling into manhood is an essential element of a father's role in affirming his son. Some men feel incapable of affirming their sons because they themselves never received full affirmation from their own fathers. It's hard to give away what we do not possess.

Jon shares a story of some dads at CITR who didn't know what to do: "The summer before last, we had a profound experience of speaking affirmations into the lives of a couple of the fathers who admitted they felt inadequate to speak words of affirmation to their sons, having never received this from their fathers. In fact, they shared they didn't really feel like men themselves. We gathered around these men, prayed for them, and spoke affirmations to them—that they were welcome in the company of men. We encouraged them that they would be able to call their sons up to manhood, even at the same time as they were 'fathering themselves.'"

Our adolescent sons desperately need our affirmation, acceptance, and affection. We dads need to affirm our sons as they make the critical transition to becoming a man. Even we dads who were never affirmed or accepted by our fathers can learn to give what we did not receive. It's a way we father ourselves and promote our own healing at the same time we love our boys. I'll say more about that in the second section of this book.

Real-Life Example

My son's rite-of-passage into manhood marked a milestone not only in his life but also in my own. I've chosen to share this intimate experience to give you one example of how a dad initiated his son into his manhood. I don't write the following as a model for you to follow. You will create your own experience. This is just one example. It's what I created for one of my teenage sons as he entered into young adulthood. I share this experience anonymously simply to protect my son's identity, per his request.

Because of my extensive readings, I was aware of the need boys have to be initiated into their manhood by their fathers, welcomed into the community of men, and given a sense of their maturing masculinity as young men—something a mother, nor any other woman nor group of women, can ever do. I wanted to create a unique experience for my son.

I was inspired by the Jewish Tradition of Bar-Mitzvahs and Bat-Mitzvahs in which the Jewish community recognizes thirteen-year-old boys and girls as sons and daughters of the commandment (the Jewish Law), welcoming them into the community of adult Jews. I searched through books and on the Internet for real-life examples of initiation rites that I could use as models for something that would make sense in our culture and for my son. However, I turned up little specific information.[41] I decided to craft our own celebration.

For this once-in-a-lifetime experience, we spent two days at a golf academy at Barren River Lake State Resort Park in Kentucky. It was marvelous. The group of golf students was limited to four and only two showed up, so my son received lots of personal attention. But that was just the beginning.

On the special evening of the initiation, I shared with my son a book about human development and anatomy, with some pictures of male and female reproductive organs. We talked in an age-appropriate way about significant changes in a young man's body: why the penis gets hard and bigger when touched, how testicles begin to produce semen and sperm, and how a man and a woman make a baby. We talked about what an ejaculation is and how it would happen soon, either as my son touched himself or at night as he slept. I was forthright, and my son, intrigued, had a big smile on his face at times. He asked a few questions. Then I said, "And this is up to you, Buddy, but if it's okay with you, I'd like to know when this happens for you the first time. We can talk about it as two men." My son thought that was great and said he'd let me know.

We also looked at a series of seven pictures that showed the development of an infant boy to an old man. I asked my son to sort these pictures into two groups. He put the first three (baby, toddler, child) together in the first group and the last four (teen, adult, middle age, old age) in the second group. This helped my son understand his rite of passage: moving from being a boy to becoming a man.

Then we went to dinner. We were quiet and tired after two long days of great golf. I asked, "What are you thinking about?"

He answered with a smile and said, "I'm just so excited about tonight."

We went back to the room and watched the original *Lion King* movie together, lying close to each other on the bed, my arm around him. We noted the beautiful relationship between the Lion King, Mufasa, and his beloved Simba, who would one day become King himself. My son and I talked about Simba becoming an adolescent and a "man," as he prepared to become King—then once he was King, how he had his own cub who would one day become King in Simba's place (the circle of life). My son loved how Mufasa (from the stars in the sky) reminded Simba, "Remember who you are. You are my son. Remember." And how Rafiki told Simba, "Mufasa is still alive. He is alive in you."

Afterwards, we walked down to the calm lake. It was getting dark, but the summer air was still warm. We sat on the shore and talked. I shared with my son that I had given him what he needed most from me during the first phase of his life—what all boys need most from their dads—to know that he was my beloved son, that I loved him, and that I wanted him and delighted in him. I said, "And I think you know that, don't you?"

He smiled, looking intently at me, listening to every word, and absorbing every moment of this experience.

I then said, "But now, as you pass into this second phase of your life, as you become a young man tonight, there is another kind of affirmation you'll need from me. You'll always be my beloved son, but now you need to know something more—all boys and girls need to know this—you need to know that I believe you have what it takes to make it in this world—to become whatever you choose to be and to accomplish whatever you desire to do. My belief in you—that you have what it takes—will inspire you and give you confidence in yourself. This will be the affirmation I give to you repeatedly throughout your adult life, and particularly in these next few years of your young manhood."

I explained to my son that I was now going to lead him through a symbolic rite of passage marked by an experience of baptism (from a Greek word meaning *to dip or to place into*). We prepared ourselves for this beautiful experience—just being in that moment together. We looked out at the peaceful lake. It was almost completely dark, no lights anywhere to be seen. Then I said solemnly, "It's time."

We walked into the water together, holding hands. We walked until we were nearly chest deep for my son. I turned to face him, and I said, "You are my beloved son in whom I am so well pleased. You have been my little boy for many years, and my big boy more recently. Tonight, I recognize that you have become a young man. As I lower you into this water, we're saying good-bye to the big boy. When I raise you up, I'm welcoming you as a young man into your manhood and inviting you into the company of men."

I lowered my son down, saying, "Good-bye, big boy." Then I raised him out of the water, saying, "Hello, young man."

We embraced tightly without saying a word. Then I moved my son away from me slightly and put my hands on his shoulders and gazed into his eyes as I said, "You have become a man tonight, a young man in whom I have complete confidence that you have everything you will need to make it in this world. I believe in you. I will support, assist, and strengthen you in any way you need me as you grow into your manhood and enjoy the company of men the rest of your life."

We hugged each other again, and we walked back to the shore, holding hands in a sacred silence.

We dried off, got dressed, and walked back up the long hill to our room. My son was happy and talkative the entire way. We reveled in this moment we would never forget.

Back in our room, my son excitedly opened the gift I had brought. He took off the wrapping paper to find a 24-by-36-inch poster of a daddy lion lying down with his head high and his little cub cuddled up against his chest. On the back of it, I had written out a special affirmation for my son that ended this way:

"May this wonderful image of a great lion and his cub forever serve as a symbolic reminder to you of this rite-of-passage blessing. For the first thirteen years of your life, I have been the great father lion, and you were my much-adored little cub. Today, you begin your journey toward becoming a great lion yourself. One day, you will have cubs to father—to care for and affirm. I love you, my son, and I believe in you. You start your journey to manhood today. Welcome to the company of men."

This poster hangs in my son's bedroom still today.

This initiation was one of the most meaningful experiences of my life as a father—giving like this to my son. I suppose I will know better in the years ahead what this experience was like for my son, when I am able to hear from him as a grown man how he reflects back upon this rite-of-passage baptism.

I offer our experience only as an example in broad-stroke terms. I'm not suggesting that you need to do what I did. I'm only offering this as one example of a rite-of-passage experience you can create for your children as they pass from being children to becoming adults.

My son's rite of passage to becoming a man was an exceptionally meaningful and intimate experience for us. I have one more son to affirm when he becomes a young man. I suspect I'll create a different experience for him when his time comes. But I do know I'll do something to mark and honor the moment and to affirm him the way I have his older brothers. I hope you will too for your children.

Prepare for Rite-of-Passage Events

- ▸ Plan your affirmation carefully.
- ▸ Think about what your children might be experiencing, not just the event itself, but what they might be feeling. Ask them. Then plan your affirmation accordingly.
- ▸ Paint a bright picture of their future.
- ▸ Tell and show them how proud you are of who they're becoming and what they've accomplished—and how much you love them.
- ▸ Be sure to communicate that you believe they have what it takes to make it.
- ▸ Share your confidence in who they are and what they are capable of achieving.

Dads, in this chapter, I've given you a sampling of the many rites of passage our children might experience throughout their lives. There are others I have not mentioned. Look for rites of passage, plan your affirmation accordingly, and give it with joy and pride, without reserve and with much affection. It will be powerfully meaningful not just in the moment, but it may shape your child's future and create positive, lifelong memories. What a privilege we have as dads to impact our children forever.

11   Giving What You Never Received

WHAT IF WE NEVER received from our own fathers the affirmation we needed to become men? In their book *The Blessing,* authors John Trent and Gary Smalley caution, "If you never heard words of love and acceptance, expect to struggle with speaking them yourself."[42]

It's hard to give away what we do not possess and have not experienced.

If this is true for you, as it was for me, then seeking your own healing will make a huge difference as to who you become as a man and father, and how full you feel to affirm your children. If you're anything like me—a son who longed for but never received my father's affirmation, acceptance, and affection—then with me you may need to attend to your own wounded heart.

Part of healing will likely mean seeking a father substitute who can affirm you now. A father substitute is usually an older man who will affirm you and accept you and share special words of hope and belief for your future, as Cory Ishida did for me. Another part of healing will be participating with other men in a healing journey in some sort of small group in which you share experiences, encourage, and affirm one another. And an additional element of healing will be learning how to affirm ourselves—to re-father ourselves as we learn to father and affirm our own children. I address these things in the next section of this book, "Healing a Father Wound."

If you don't know how to affectionately affirm and fully accept your children, if you've never done that, or if you've tried and it felt awkward or forced or phony, that's okay. Learning to affirm our sons and daughters—if we have never done so—is not really all that different from acquiring any other new skill later in life. Imagine taking up golf for the first time. It takes many hours of repeated practice and some good instruction to become any good at it. But it's really a fun game when you get some good instruction, take the time to practice, and improve your skill level.

> It may take some time and practice to learn
> how to affectionately affirm and accept
> your children and feel at ease doing so.

Perhaps it will take some encouragement and coaching for you to become good at and comfortable with affirming your kids, but it's worth it. Giving or withholding your affirmation will impact your children's lives forever.

Here's What To Do

The first and all-important step is to dedicate yourself to affectionately affirming and accepting your children repeatedly, throughout their lives, in the day-to-day experiences of life, at special life moments, and at rites of passage. Then try it. Try it again, and again, and again. Practice it. Really work at becoming a great dad who has mastered the three A's of great fathering: affirmation, acceptance, and affection. Don't ever give up. Over time, it will become more natural.

For dads who have not affirmed their children, just be honest with them about your failure to do so until now as well as your new commitment to figure out how to affirm them from now on. Say to them something like, "I didn't get affectionate affirmation and acceptance from my dad growing up and didn't even realize it until recently. I now see how much I've missed it and how much I want to learn to give that to you. I wish I had done so earlier, but I promise to affectionately affirm and accept you from now on—the rest of your life. This isn't easy for me, though I really want to learn. Try to be patient with me."

Honestly admitting something like this to your kids while sharing your desire to affirm them will be an amazing gift of affirmation in itself. It will speak to them of your love for them and your longing to grow as a great dad. They'll know how special they are to you when you honestly reveal your own wound and lack of affirmation as well as your fresh commitment to communicate your love to them. Make sure to follow through on your very good and stated intentions.

> **Even if our fathers, to this day, have not affirmed us, we can still learn to affirm our children.**

And we must. Your children need your affirmation, acceptance, and affection just as badly as you needed your father's—and perhaps still do. Let's give what we may not have received. In giving, we will find love returning to us as well. It's part of healing. It's a big part of how we become the great dads we want to be and our children need us to be.

Some Practical Suggestions

Try these, and make up your own.

- ▸ Tell them daily something you see in them that is positive. Say it out loud. A spoken affirmation is clear and powerful. If at all possible, touch your kids while you affirm them.

- ▸ Tell them every day how much you love them and how glad you are that you are their dad. Something like, "I love you so much, my son/daughter. I'm so happy that you are my child and that I get to be your dad. I love you, and I'm so, so proud of you." If you have a daughter, tell her often how competent and beautiful that you think she is and that you'll love her always. Affectionate touch is vital. For your son, tell him you're proud of him and believe in him and that you'll love him forever.

- ▸ For no apparent reason and at seemingly random times, hug them, hold them, and touch them in some appropriate and affectionate, even playful way to show your love for them and help them *feel* it.

- ▸ Affirm them nightly at bedtime, especially when they're young. If you pray, you might pray something like, "May God bless you and keep you and show his great and tender love for you this night, and always. And may his peace be with you. You are my beloved son/daughter (use your child's name here), and I am so well pleased in you. I will never leave you. I will never forsake you. For you are my son/daughter, and I'll love you forever, no matter what."

- ▸ If you don't pray, you can express the picture you have of a bright future for them and why you see that. Be as specific as you can. Point out character qualities, interests, and skills you see in them and some ways you can imagine them using these to benefit others, perhaps even ways to build a career out of them or start a business. Help them feel the bright picture you have of their future and your pride in who they

are becoming, what they have accomplished, decisions they've
made, and people they've helped.

▸ Make the most of special moments in their lives and make
them even more special by adding your affectionate affirmation to the moment.

▸ Think deeply about milestone life transitions in your children's lives—rites of passage. Plan a special affirmation to
mark the occasion and imprint their soul with your delight
in them and love for them.

It's Never Too Late

Neil Chethik writes about sons and fathers. That was the focus of the
300 in-depth surveys and seventy interviews he conducted as research
for his book *FatherLoss: How Sons of All Ages Come to Terms with the
Deaths of Their Dads*. Yet much of what he says can apply to daughters
and their fathers as well. This is especially true when he encourages
older fathers to keep fathering or, in some cases, to begin fathering
their now grown sons.

He writes: "Even when a positive father-son connection fails to
occur in the son's *childhood*, there are usually opportunities to com-
pensate later. Another lesson I learned from the sons I interviewed
was that fathering does not really end when a son is twenty-one, or
forty-one, or even sixty-one. Throughout our lives, right up until
the time of our deaths, we fathers have opportunities to deepen our
relationships with our sons. One way a father can enhance his relationship with his son is by blessing the younger man."[43]

Chethik illustrates this from his own life. He shares the impact
of receiving his father's affirmation, what he calls "the direct result of
his respect for me," when he was twenty-seven years old.

> He'd said: "I want to tell you now how proud I am of you,
> of the choices you've made, of the life you've created."
> At the time, his father had just died, and my father was

poignantly aware of having missed his dad's affirmation in his own life. My father's blessing was especially important to me because I was concerned that I'd disappointed him. He'd put me through college, and now, five years into my career, I'd quit a good job with no plan as to what I'd do next. When my father told me he was proud of the choices I'd made, I took it to mean that he supported me in my decision to stop and reevaluate my career direction. I felt the pressure lift and began to trust myself to make the right next steps.[44]

It's never too late to affectionately affirm and accept your children, no matter how long it has been since you've done so or even if you never have. If your kids are older now, it's never too late to extend to them your affirmation of who they are and the direction of their life. Look for ways to show you admire, respect, and are proud of them. Tell them in the warmest way you can. It can make all the difference for them—and for you as well.

Real Life Example

Miguel was a thirty-year-old incarcerated father when I met him. He had spent most of the last ten years in and out of prison. During the few months at a time he was released, he got three different women pregnant. He had no relationship with any of his children. He had never even met them. Each of them had been born after he had been rearrested and locked up again.

Miguel shared his heartbreaking story with me one evening, choking back tears as he spoke about his own father. His dad wasn't around much when Miguel was growing up. He too had spent much of his adult life in and out of prison. When he was out, he never had a positive thing to say. He told Miguel repeatedly that he was no good, that he was stupid, that he would never amount to much, and that he would probably end up in prison just like his old man. Those words became a life path for Miguel as he absorbed his father's wounding negativity.

Miguel and I had many conversations about his children whom he'd abandoned. As the months passed, I observed a softening taking place. Miguel came to me one afternoon and asked me how he could reach out to his children to begin a relationship with them. For the first time in his life, he wanted to be a dad. He wanted to give something to his children he had never given: himself, his love, and his masculine presence.

I told Miguel he would first have to contact the mothers of his children to restore some relationship and trust with them. He began writing to each of them every week. He shared what he was learning and how he was growing, healing, and changing. He told them that he wanted to begin fulfilling his responsibility of being a father. He also promised the mothers that upon his release, he would take responsibility for providing some financial support for them as they raised his children. Miguel was growing up and becoming a good, more responsible man.

After many months of letters, one of the mothers came to visitation so that Miguel could meet his oldest son. What a day that was! Miguel had trouble sleeping for days before the visit because he was so excited and nervous. When Miguel met Juan, then six years old, Juan was wearing his Little League baseball uniform. He wanted his dad to see him in it because he had been told that Miguel loved baseball. He wanted his dad to feel proud of him.

Miguel told Juan how glad he was to see him, that he loved him, and that he was so proud of him. It wasn't fifteen minutes before Juan had jumped into Miguel's lap, given him a great big neck hug, and said, "Daddy, I love you." Juan asked his dad to read him a story. He'd brought a baseball book with him. Miguel was thrilled as he shared with me and then with the entire PEP class what happened for him that day as he restored his relationship with one of his children.

After I taught the men of PEP about a father wound and the power of receiving or withholding affirmation, acceptance, and affection,

Miguel approached me, stood silently before me for a moment, then broke into sobs of anguish as he told me he knew his father didn't love him and was ashamed of him. I wrapped my arms around him, held him tightly, and even rocked him as I spoke words of affirmation and acceptance to him myself.

After Miguel composed himself a bit, he shared with me that he had invited his entire family to his graduation ceremony from PEP the next month. He had even invited the three women who were the mothers of his children. All three said they would come and bring the children: Juan (six), Rosa (five), and Antonio (three). His mother, sister, and two brothers were also coming. His mother wrote to him, however, that his father refused to attend. She apologized that he would not be there for Miguel's special day.

The day of graduation soon arrived. Miguel was thrilled to meet Rosa and Antonio and to see Juan again. He had written many letters to all three children, and they had sent him cards, photos of themselves, and pictures they had drawn. Miguel was excited and nervous. At the same time, I could sense a deep sadness in him. I asked him about this and he said, "All I've ever wanted was for my father to be proud of me and to accept me. I know I've disappointed him and made a mess of my life, but I've spent the last six months growing and changing. I'm proud of who I'm becoming and what I've accomplished in this program. I wanted to show my dad what I'm making of my life now. I'm becoming a good dad. I've created a business plan I know I'll be successful at when I'm released. And I'm becoming a man of character. I wanted my dad to be here, to see what I've done and who I'm becoming. I wanted to make him proud, but he doesn't want to see me. Why can't he love me like I love my own kids? I just want to hear him say once he loves me and he's proud of me." Miguel stopped speaking and started crying. I understood his pain.

That night at graduation, when I stood before the men at the end of the program, I invited them to come forward so I could affirm them with love the way I speak to my own children—like a father.

I then invited their families to come forward too. I was delighted to see Miguel's children run forward to be with him. He scooped up all three of them at once and held them tightly as he burst into tears of joy. Then his mother, his sister, and his brothers came to stand with him and support him.

I noticed an older man stand up at the back of the room. He slowly walked toward the stage, found Miguel, and stood behind him as I spoke and affirmed the men.

After the affirmation, I dispersed the crowd for refreshments. I found Miguel in the crowd. He grabbed me and hugged me so tightly I almost lost my breath. He stepped back while still grabbing my shoulders with both of his hands. He was radiant, with a huge smile on his face. He said, "Keith, my father was here tonight. He came. He stood with me during your affirmation and halfway through I felt his hand on my shoulder. When you were done speaking, I turned and looked in his face. He had tears in his eyes as he spoke to me in Spanish. He said, 'Miguel, I don't know what to say. I never imagined anyone in our family making anything of their life. But you have. You have become the man I always wanted to be. You're a better father than I ever was, a better man. I'm proud of you, Miguel, my son.'

> Dads, it's never too late. Set your children free
> with your affirmation, acceptance, and affection.

At last, the affirmation, acceptance, and affection Miguel had hungered for all his life. At thirty, he finally heard his father tell him he was proud of him and loved him.

Affectionately Affirm and Accept Your Children

What your children really need is to know and feel that you are proud of them, love them, accept them, and picture a bright and beautiful future for them. They need to know they belong, are valued, and wanted. They need you to touch and hold them in a warm and meaningful way as you speak your affirmations to them.

It's never too late.

It's always meaningful.

It's part of becoming a great dad.

It's the gift of a lifetime to your children.

12　You Can Do This

IT TAKES TIME TO BUILD great relationships with your kids—lots of time. Missteps and mistakes along the way are normal—we should expect them. I'm grateful for the Jewish Proverb that says, "Love covers a multitude of transgressions." Whenever you've failed to be the dad you want to be, remember this reality, be thankful you love your kids, and keep moving forward.

> You are still your child's father!
> No one else ever can or will take
> your place of honor and influence.

I've made many suggestions in this section of the book. It's possible you may feel discouraged. Some might feel it's too big a leap to get from where you are today to where I'm encouraging you to be. Don't let that be a problem. I'm painting a picture of the ideal to inspire you toward it. I'm not offering all this as the norm. If you fall short, as I do, well, join the club.

Don't be disheartened, Dad. No matter where you are today, set your sights on what you've read in this section of the book about affirming, accepting, and being affectionate with your children as a target. Aim and fire away. If you miss on nine shots, maybe the tenth will hit. It doesn't have to be a bulls-eye. Really. Just pick out one or two suggestions and begin there. (See appendix A for a complete list of action steps). When that strategy becomes more natural, then try something else. Consider the practices and examples I share throughout the book as tools in your toolbox. When you need a specific tool, you'll know where to find it. Grab it and use it. Next time, grab another.

Some dads get discouraged because they regret fathering decisions they've made or because they no longer live full time with their kids or because they feel too wounded themselves to provide their affirmation, acceptance, and affection for their children. Maybe you feel you've been anything but a blessing to your kids. Perhaps you're incarcerated or addicted or debilitated in some other way. Maybe your kids live with their mom and possibly a stepfather. Please allow these words to sink in:

No matter where you are, no matter what limitations you currently experience or mistakes you've made, no matter how far away from your goal you feel, you can still grow as a father to become the best dad you can be. You can become a great dad: being affirming, accepting, and affectionate with your children.

You really can:
- Give verbal and written affirmations.
- Provide unconditional and unending acceptance.
- Share spoken and physical affection.

You can do this! All of us as infants had to learn to crawl before we could walk and walk before we could run. All you have to do is to take the next step in front of you. You don't have to do all the things I've written at once. Pick one of the three crucial fathering skills and do just one at a time. It's okay to make slow progress and lots of mistakes. We learn that way.

You have great power as a father to positively influence your children. Even if you've not used that power well thus far, or perhaps even been aware of it, you can begin anew today. All dads possess immense influence to shape their kids lives by applying these three crucial fathering skills.

Together, we can do this. You can do this. By learning affirmation, acceptance, and affection skills, working at them through repetition, and sharing in the journey with some other dads who are learning and practicing too, you really can become the great dad you want to be—perhaps the dad you wish you had.

Encouragement from a Single Dad

On fatherapprentice.com, Courtney Stubbert, father of two, posted a blog titled "Good Enough is Good. Enough." He wrote,

> **If you think you have to be awesome all the time you are setting yourself up for failure** (and whiskey; and cheap whiskey at that). There is nobody on the planet that can do all the things a parent has to do with a partner, let alone by yourself, and think it will be done with humor, grace, and smiles all the time. Some days you'll be lucky if it's even that way 50% of the time.

> And this is how I know my "good enough" is good enough. No matter what I do wrong, at some point in the evening my son will still say, "Dad I just love you. You're the best." To which I humbly reply, "Thanks bud, I love you too."

> **Kids are amazing at loving you back despite your faults.** They live in the moment and as long as you're not crazy

or really blowing it in a serious or illegal way, they just want to know that you are there no matter what.

So that is what I do. Be there no matter what, be honest, be as present as possible, apologize when I need to and always, always, always tell them something I like about them.[45]

Thanks, Courtney. These are great words with which to conclude this section of the book on sharing affirmation, acceptance, and affection with our kids. Your words give hope to our fathering journeys.

Dads, you can do this!

Part II

Healing a
Father Wound

"My sister has always said that one of her jobs
in the family has been to remember everything
that's happened along the way. 'So I can remind
you in case you forget' is what she says. Not that
I've forgotten anything. It's just that up until
now, I've had to block a lot of it out. But no more.
If I want to be the Daddy I promised myself
as a child that I was going to be, it's time to go
back there and do the remembering myself."

Dwyane Wade, NBA Champion, in his book
A Father First: How My Life Became Bigger Than Basketball

13   Father Hunger

FATHER HUNGER is a term many psychologists, authors, and poets use to describe the universal and lifelong yearning children have for their fathers. Sometimes loving dads satisfy that hunger. Other times, children continue to yearn when disengaged fathers fail to meet their need. Some starve from complete lack of fathering or abandonment through death, divorce, or desertion. Fatherlessness leaves children hungry—craving their dad's affirmation, acceptance, and loving affection. Father-hungry children tend not to grow up to be healthy, well-adjusted, and happy adults. A host of studies link fatherlessness to many serious social problems. Children from fatherless homes account for:

- 63 percent of youth suicides.
- 71 percent of pregnant teenagers.
- 90 percent of all homeless and runaway children.
- 70 percent of juveniles in state-operated institutions.
- 85 percent of all youth who exhibit behavior disorders.
- 80 percent of rapists motivated with displaced anger.
- 71 percent of all high school dropouts.
- 75 percent of all adolescents in chemical abuse centers.
- 85 percent of all youths sitting in prison.[46]

Clinical child development researchers Frank Furstenberg and Kathleen Harris reveal that more important than a father's presence or even his living at home is how close a child feels to his or her father. That feeling of closeness, they argue, is most predictably associated with positive life outcomes for the child even twenty-five years later.

Based on these findings, Dr. Kyle Pruett notes, "Children who feel a closeness to their father are twice as likely as those who do not to enter college or find stable employment after high school, 75 percent less likely to have a teen birth, 80 percent less likely to spend time in jail, and half as likely to experience multiple depression symptoms."[47]

A study in the *Journal of the American Medical Association* confirmed that "doing lots of activities together is not the crucial variable in the relationship between parent and child; rather, it is a *sense of connectedness*."[48]

> Ultimately, it's how close children feel to
> their dads that makes all the difference as
> to how satisfied their father hunger is.

Children hunger for their missing fathers all their lives—even as adults. Many grown men still hunger for their fathers, as I did. Separation from one's children can exacerbate the longing. Gail Sheehy, in her insightful book *Understanding Men's Passages,* reports that "Father hunger is particularly sharp among men who have lost close contact with their children through divorce. Often, the relationship with their own fathers was distant, mechanical, or downright intimidating, and they have reproduced much the same pattern with their own children. The longer they allow the relationship with their children to lapse, the more difficult they will find it to break that pattern, to feel comfortable hugging and laughing and crying together."[49]

Like our physical hunger for food, father hunger never ultimately goes away, even when it is momentarily satisfied. We continue to hunger for more of our father's love.

Father hunger is evidence of how much dads matter to their children.

It's satisfying when children feel their dads' love on a regular basis. It leaves a painful ache and emptiness, however, when dads are absent or inadequate—when they don't express their love or their children don't feel it. One of the most common and significant causes of fathers leaving their children hungry and wounded is that the fathers are still hungry and wounded themselves. Without knowing it and without wanting to, we reproduce the wounding in our children that still exists in our own soul.

The more self-aware a man can become of any father wounding in his own life, and the more healing he will pursue, the better father he will become to his own children—more free to love and affirm them the way he wishes his father had been able to do for him.

That's what this second section of the book is about. If you experienced some unfulfilled longing for your father, this section will help you identify that and show you a path toward healing. If you don't need this section for your own healing, it will help you better understand the experience of many other men and prepare you to be a better friend, colleague, or partner to them.

Father hunger describes the universal and lifelong yearning children have for their fathers.

---

14   Father Wounding

*"Our fathers profoundly influence us, more than most of us care
to acknowledge. I have noticed that when middle-aged sons
speak of their fathers (dead or alive), there is often hesitancy
in their voices, a telling silence full of muted emotion."*

— Charles Scull, Ph.D.[50]

IN MOST OF MY TEACHING, I speak to men as fathers to their
children. In this section of the book, we'll remember ourselves as
sons to our fathers when we were young. In the first section about
sharing affirmation, acceptance, and affection with our children, we
took a forward look—how to shape our children to help them become
all *they* can be. Here, we'll take a backward look to discover what
might be preventing us from being all *we* can be.

Ken Canfield, fatherhood researcher and founder of the National
Center for Fathering, writes in his book *The Heart of a Father*, "The
yearning of many men today to become good fathers is rooted in our
past—we are all children who want our fathers."[51] We'll take this
backward look in order to move forward.

Examining our relationship to our own fathers is one of the most vital—but often ignored—steps in becoming the dads we aspire to be now. Canfield puts it plainly, "I believe it's critical that we who are fathers deal with our hearts in order to connect with our children."

Yet the hearts of many fathers are aching from a wound that does not go away, though few pay attention to the pain or its effects. Many of us grew up without a father or with a dad who did not engage with us, love and affirm us, or help us grow to become men. As a result, many of us do not possess a sense of who we are as men. Many of our fathers did not model the father we long to be.

In his book *Fathers, Sons, and Daughters*, psychologist Charles Scull observes, "Fathers who are wounded are suffering. And they create children who are wounded."[52] Our desire is just the opposite; we don't want to wound our children by passing our father wound to them. We want to shape kids who are full of love, life, and joy. In order to do so, we need to be dads who possess those attributes in good measure ourselves. Healing leads us there.

**Healing and restoration are as
essential as they are freeing.**

This section of the book may not be a quick or easy read if what follows touches your father wound. This is a topic more complex than I can fully treat in this short section of this book. However, I include it as a significant introduction to this vital aspect of good fathering because it's essential that each of us takes a careful look at our own wound if we hope to become the great dads we long to be. For a fuller treatment and freeing experience, please attend one of my Healing the Father Wound workshops.

> "It's easier to build strong children
> than to repair broken men."
> — Frederick Douglas

Douglas is right—repairing broken men is immensely difficult. But thankfully, it's not impossible. As we become more skilled and healed dads, we'll shape a new generation of strong, well-adjusted, deeply loved daughters and sons.

15 Defining a Father Wound

THE TERM *father wound* has been used for many years by numerous psychologists, sociologists, authors, and poets to speak of the damage done to one's psyche (soul) by a less than adequate, absent, or damaging relationship with one's father. A significant father wound may exist because of an abusive father who was violent, alcoholic, sexually inappropriate, or verbally insulting. A dad at the other end of the spectrum—a dad who was not present in the family, either physically or emotionally—often leaves a wound. Some dads are passive or absent due to divorce, death, or a commitment to work or their own interests that takes them away from their children for substantial portions of time. There are also many dads in between those extremes who mean well but who lack the knowledge, skills, emotional resources, or their own healing to give the affirmation, attention, affection, or even time their children need.

There are as many different inadequacies in dads as there are dads. There are no perfect fathers. All fathers wound their kids in some ways, some relatively minor, easily forgiven, and forgotten, others more severe and more difficult to heal. A father wound may exist

117

because of an intentionally cruel or severely defective father, but that is not often the case.

Even the best (yet imperfect) dads inadvertently wound their children.

All dads make mistakes. Mine did, yours likely did, I certainly do, and you probably do as well. Those mistakes may hurt the children we love. It can also get much worse. Psychologists and sociologists search for terms to describe a pandemic problem: boys and girls who grow up without receiving all they need from their dads get wounded. That wound does not simply go away as we get older. If not healed, we pass the wound on to our children.[53]

Marriage and family therapist Alan Javurek, Ph.D., notes, "Estrangement between fathers and sons is a cultural phenomenon as well as a personal tragedy. This rift is so common that psychologists have developed terms such as *father hunger* and the *wounded father* in an attempt to describe the psychological and emotional states created by children's experiences of growing into adulthood while living in an emotionally conflicted or deprived relationship with their fathers."[54]

Many men are aware that something going back to their inadequate relationship with their dad affects and sometimes even cripples their attempts at fathering their children.[55] Boys who do not get what they need from their dads are less equipped to become men themselves and are less able to give to their own sons and daughters all that their children need and crave.[56] This is true of us. And it was true of our dads.[57]

This passing down of the father wound does not just go away of its own accord. Ignoring this phenomenon does not eradicate its existence. Psychologist Donald Joy writes, "Boys need their father's blessing and their fidelity to the naïve ideal of childhood idolatry. But any form of dishonesty between father and son sets an agenda of 'unfinished business' that frequently haunts the adult life of the son, often damaging his aspirations, marriage, and parenting behavior."[58]

I hope to help you begin to identify such unfinished business and to become aware of the need and process to finish it so you will not pass down your unfinished business to yet another generation.

Alcoholics Anonymous puts it this way: "What we don't pass back, we pass down." We can stop the legacy of pain by healing it in ourselves.[59] What a gift to ourselves, to our children, to our families, and to our world.

16 What Does a Father Wound Look Like?

IN A MAN'S LIFE, the father wound may appear as poor self-image or sadness as an often-present undercurrent. It may develop into a pattern of failures at work or in intimate relationships. It can emerge as pride or machismo that exists to cover up fear or feelings of inadequacy or insecurity or just not feeling loved. It may manifest in using women for sexual satisfaction that soothes the pain of rejection. It may lead to abuse of alcohol or cigarettes or another substance. It may result in depression.

Many men use the rush of adrenaline from risk taking, gambling, extreme sports or adventures, sexual pleasure, or dangerous activities including violence and war to mask pain or feelings of emptiness or worthlessness. There are countless manifestations of the father wound that distort a man's life and prevent him from feeling and acting like a mature, affirmed, and loving man.[60]

Dads also wound their daughters. There may be manifestations that are more specific to women. For example, in intimate relationships with men they may repeat the wounding experienced with their fathers. Such repeating is often the result of the craving for male affection, attention, and delight needed but not received from their fathers during their childhood and adolescence. A woman with a father wound may feel unworthy, not valued, unattractive, or incapable, lacking praise by her father for the positive antitheses of these attributes. Some wounded women overcompensate and become more masculine, dominant, and sometimes aggressively seductive in order to get back at their father through the men they conquer.

Some women feel a need to compete to show their fathers that they are capable, strong winners, what they likely believe their fathers wanted them to be. Some women attempt to assuage their disappointment and prove to their fathers they should have been loved.

My Father Wound

You already know I experienced a less than adequate relationship with my dad. I've mentioned how giving to my boys what I did not receive has been healing. To be clear, I'm going to share my journey openly to paint one picture of what healing a father wound can look like and how essential healing is to become the dads we long to be for the children we love. I do not offer my journey as the norm or a pattern all must follow. This is my story—how I found healing and freedom. I hope it inspires and empowers you to discover and pursue your own.

Due to my father's absence in my middle and later childhood, then in my adolescence, and later as an adult, I found myself repeatedly waiting and hungering for something my dad would never give me: himself—his engaged presence and loving affirmation.

I shared that my dad physically left our family when I was seven and divorced my mom when I was nine, but he had left in many ways long before. I wrote about the ongoing pattern of rejection and how I came to realize that even when my dad was alive, I felt like a fatherless son. I told the story of my father's final rejection of me as his son and how badly that hurt. Perhaps with that background, you can understand or imagine how I hungered for my father all the years of my youth, and then even as a college student and adult. It was a hunger that became a constant longing for the father I would never have.

That yearning became an ingrained pattern—a way of being—one that led to numerous problems in my young adult and later adult relationships. A psychologist I later sought help from referred to this as *repeating without remembering*. I would unknowingly repeat or unintentionally recreate this all-too-familiar experience for myself, subconsciously hoping that I would somehow this time (in the present) change it—that there would be a different outcome and I wouldn't feel the pain.

Without knowing it, I tried to change the past by controlling the present. I now know that even if I had been successful in achieving a different outcome in the present situation or relationship, it still would not heal my past, though that is the subconscious hope in such situations. This never works. This hope to heal the past by controlling the present is often not recognized by the one trying to work out his past pain. I certainly had no idea why the same issues, problems, and pain kept showing up in my relationships.

I always felt unhappy, even when present circumstances or relationships seemed to be going well. I always feared it would end because I had come to believe that I would never get what I really wanted—I'd never be happy and feel loved. Years later, I realized I did not believe I even deserved to be happy. I subconsciously recreated my feelings of sadness and father loss by creating situations in the present that played out and confirmed my false belief. I either chose inadequate relationships that confirmed the feelings I experienced inside myself or sabotaged relationships that promised something more than my broken heart could receive. In fact, I subconsciously sabotaged everything good in my life so my false belief formed by my past would become my present reality. That way, I wouldn't feel so crazy. My outer world of failed romances and professional opportunities would then match my internal feelings of sadness and loss.

After each failure in life, business, and love, I would think within myself, *See, this is how it goes for you. You'll never succeed. You'll never be loved. You'll never get what you want.* That false, limiting belief would be reinforced and grow stronger. It became my sad reality.

My life became a series of disappointments and my feelings of loneliness, sadness, and lack of love never went away. Situations, experiences, or people who made me feel loved somehow felt wrong to me—like a shoe that didn't fit. I began to avoid or resist situations and relationships that might make me happy.

It makes me sad to remember the lonely years and people I hurt along the way who did not and could not understand why they couldn't get close to me or make me feel loved. My heart resembled a black hole—nothing and no one could fill me. It never seemed to be enough. Until my wound began to heal, I couldn't allow myself to feel happy or loved. Those positive feelings were too inconsistent with my wounded heart and the false beliefs I adopted to cope with and survive my pain. Can you imagine the kind of father I would have been had I had children at this stage of my life, prior to my much-needed healing?

For the reasons I'm admitting, I couldn't sustain an intimate relationship with a woman. I always ended up feeling unloved. The relationship would wither and die, often by my own (usually subconscious) doing. I did not marry until I was nearly thirty-two years old, with still a great deal of healing and growing to do. We had our first son when I was thirty-seven.

I'm thankful I didn't become a father earlier because I would have passed my unfulfilled longing and sadness—my wound—to my sons the way my dad passed his to me. That would have broken my heart. I wanted to be a better dad to my children than my dad had been to me. I wanted to break the chain of misery that existed as a pattern in my father's family.[61] I wanted to leave to my sons a different legacy of love.

If you're reading this prior to having children and recognize a father wound in your own soul, may I suggest doing some significant healing work as I describe in the chapters that follow before welcoming children into your life. Your healing will be a gift to your kids before you even meet them because it will free you to be a better, more present, and loving father than you could have been prior to your substantial healing. I'm not advocating waiting until you are perfectly healed. Perfect healing is an unrealistic dream, but substantial healing is possible and does set us free.

> Substantial healing helps us become the men,
> husbands, and fathers we hope to be.

If you recognize your wound but already have children, then you'll have to manage both at the same time. That is not an easy task but it is doable. You can heal your own wound while learning to affirm, accept, and be affectionate with your kids. You can do this. And I will help you.

17 One Healing Journey Illustrated

I BEGAN MY HEALING JOURNEY when I turned twenty-nine years old. It took me until then to see the unhealthy patterns in my relationships. I kept trying to make relationships work and to pick better people (so I thought), but the same results kept resurfacing. I never felt loved. What the women in my life gave me never felt like enough to make up for the sorrow I felt, the emptiness I experienced, or the longing for my father's love and approval.

However, I had not yet recognized the real issue. I blamed the women for not being loving enough. I became lonelier and more discouraged about the direction my life took. Very slowly, through the help of some close friends, one a psychologist, I admitted the problems in my outside world—my work and relationships—were actually manifestations of pain from my inside world—the thoughts, beliefs, and feelings I had acquired about life and myself.

I gradually accepted I had to make peace with my past. I needed to figure out the thoughts and feelings *inside* me if I wanted things *outside* to change. I began to read books about psychological wounding and healing, soul care, and how the mind works. I made my first appointment with a psychologist. I entered therapy with some hope for the future and a great deal of anxiety. I felt scared to explore and feel all the sadness within.

I spent the next two years in therapy, much of it twice a week, sometimes more, working toward and later through my past pain and present difficulties. At the beginning, I felt frightened and out of control by the strength of the feelings I experienced and the significant grief that surfaced. I often wanted to cry, but I feared that if I started I might never stop. And of course, I felt all that male macho crap about men not crying. My fear and confusion centered on how I would function at work if I began to feel the pain I had ignored for so long. It wasn't much of a life I was living, but at least I knew how to function and cope. If I got into that world of internal pain I thought all hell might break loose. I felt scared.

I told my therapist that I imagined a dam inside me holding back an immense amount of water (my pain): if I poked holes in the dam, the whole structure might collapse, and a torrent would break through. I couldn't believe my therapist calmly asked, "And what would be wrong with that?"

I thought, *It's he who needs therapy. Doesn't he understand how frightening that would be? Doesn't he get how overwhelmed I feel? Can't he recognize I won't be able to function at work or in life if I fall apart?* He did, of course. I now understand his wisdom. His question gently led me to face my fears—to realize that the fear of pain is usually greater than the pain itself.

He assured me that after many years of controlling my grief, I would be able to stop it if it got too intense. I sort of, kind of, a little bit believed him. But not much. It took me months to test this process. When I finally did, a little bit at a time, I found that sorrow is not nearly as frightening, overwhelming, nor devastating as the fear of it portends.

In fact, when my grief began to surface, I did control how much of it I felt, just as my therapist figured. After many years of denying my sadness, I had become quite skilled at shutting it down as needed. I discovered something liberating about beginning to feel grief, a bit at a time. I soon realized it required more energy to keep grief down and hidden than to let it surface. I experienced a truth I now cling to—pain on the way in is wounding; pain on the way out is healing.

As I felt in the present the wounds of my past and identified them as such, I actually started feeling a bit better. As I slowly let my pain surface, it began to dissipate. When I held my pain in, denied its presence, blamed it on someone or something else, refused to face it, embrace it, name it, and feel it—and believe me, I spent years doing all of that—my wound just kept hurting. That's how my sadness from the past continued to make me despondent in the present. And it's why my wound leaked out into all my present experiences and relationships.

I slowly—and I mean very slowly, over a one-year period—began to believe that to explore, identify, feel, and release my pain would be healing and freeing. I eventually stopped being scared of it. I began to view my wound as an unanticipated friend. I came to believe that if I would feel my sadness and loss, it would lead me to the better and happier places I wanted to be and the more loving and intimate relationships I wanted to experience.

> I found what the twelve-step programs
> teach: "The only way to the other
> side of grief is through it."

As I finally accepted my wound and felt it, I started to become free of how sad I felt all the time and of how my wound poisoned my life and relationships.

18 The Healing Process – Step #1: Identifying a Father Wound

I CAN'T DO JUSTICE in these few chapters to all I experienced while substantially healing my father wound. What I can and will share are the stages through which I passed, with some introductory thoughts to explain them, as they unfolded before me.

As my courage grew and my fear abated, I followed a process that eventually led to my substantial healing and freed me to become the father I dreamed of being. This is my wish for you. I describe the steps I took in this chapter and in the five chapters that follow. I'm not suggesting that everyone must heal the way I did. One size does not fit all. There are pieces of my journey, however, that are common to healing. Although your process may look different—whether shorter or longer, less or more intense, in this order or another—there may be lessons you can learn and apply from my experience. I provide my story to pique your curiosity and to inspire you to look into your own soul to see what sort of wounding, if any, you may need to heal.

All of us experience some wounding. For those fortunate enough to have had good or even great dads, that limited wound may not cause obvious pain or significant problems later in life. For others, we experience a grief that is often unidentified but nonetheless present and affective.

Psychologist Charles Scull recognizes the universal nature of father wounding since all fathers are human. He writes, "Fathers seem to evoke a certain ambivalence. We love them, we hate them, we want them, we reject them. We desperately yearn to find some common ground of connection with them. The father-child relationship can be difficult because fathers were a part of our lives when we were the most vulnerable. And, inevitably, they made mistakes. They were invariably too hard or too soft, too distant or too overpowering."[62]

Yet identifying and admitting this universal reality in our lives is as rare as it is difficult. Perhaps it is rare for that reason. Donald Joy writes, "Father loss, whether by death, abandonment, desertion, or divorce, evokes a deep grief. Yet sometimes grief is short-circuited or choked, and remains in the denial stage."[63] Mine did for years.

As a child, I believed I had the perfect father. Later I learned that many psychologists believe that many children *have* to believe such a fantasy, especially when dads are far from adequate. Though my dad left, my child's mind and need figured it must not have been his fault or due to his problems. There had to be some other reason.

It would be frightening to believe my father was not a good man or that he didn't love me or that he wanted to leave. I chose—as many children do in such situations—not to believe any of that. I created alternate explanations. I made up other reasons for my dad abandoning me, and our family. My make-believe excuses for my dad included blaming myself, and my mom—she must have driven him away—which, as you might imagine, created all sorts of problems in my relationship with her, and later with other women. I adopted my father's belief—women are great for sex, but you cannot live with a woman.

I had no idea what I had done to make my dad want to leave me. I wasn't a bad kid. I understood years later that I subconsciously concluded, *Something must be terribly wrong with me, or surely my dad would have loved me and stayed with me. That's what dads of good kids do.*

Many psychologists refer to this common childhood way of coping with the loss of a father as an *internalizing of blame*.[64] To place responsibility where it belonged, with my dad, to embrace the reality that he chose to leave, was too painful. I needed him too much to see him as flawed. To have an inadequate dad with his own set of significant problems was not safe; that reality would decimate security. In order to keep Dad strong, powerful, and good in my childhood imagination, I had to shift responsibility elsewhere—to Mom, and to myself.[65]

Please recognize my purpose in sharing all this is not to blame my dad, nor to encourage you to blame yours. Blame is not a part of this discussion, nor is it part of healing. I had to recognize and honestly identify that some of the pain in my soul and some of the problems in my life and relationships were the residual effects of a father wound. My dad may have meant well, but he wasn't equipped by his dad to be all I needed him to be. And he made choices that made him an inadequate father.

As long as all this went unidentified, as long as I ignored, denied, or just didn't know this, it influenced me powerfully. Psychologist Jerrold Lee Shapiro writes, "Any man who is unaware of the important influences in his own father's history is likely to carry around emotional baggage that serves him poorly. Until he understands the source of such emotional reactions, he will be inordinately controlled by them."[66] And these reactions affect all our intimate relationships, especially with our partners and our children. It's imperative that we identify this wound in order to embrace, grieve, and heal it.[67]

> We cannot set out to heal a wound
> if we haven't yet properly identified it,
> or if we deny its existence.

Gaining understanding must be the first step toward healing. We have to identify the real issues if we hope to effectively resolve them. The key is identifying which of our life and relationship problems in the present may in fact be rooted in a father wound from the past.

Seeing a competent therapist was an essential and enlightening part of my identification process. I had to recognize that my sadness, loneliness, and at times overwhelming feelings of not being loved were the indicators that something more was going on beneath the surface of my life and my present relationships. I had to acknowledge that there was pain from the past leaking into the present and begin to identify what that pain was about—my father wound.

An Inward Look

- Are you aware of sadness in your life that does not seem to go away?
- Do you long for the affirmation of other men (a boss, friends, co-workers)?
- Do you desire to be affirmed by women?
- Does it sometimes feel like there is a hole in your heart or that something important is missing inside you?
- Does criticism really sting?
- Do you lack confidence?
- Do you fear failure?
- Are you having trouble feeling close to your partner or your children?
- Is it difficult for you to express your love freely, or sometimes even to feel it?

If you answered yes to several of those questions, it is worth exploring the possible presence of a father wound—the result of an inadequate relationship with your father that left you unfulfilled, still longing for the affirmation, acceptance, and affection he was not able to give. If that wound exists, you can only heal it once you clearly identify its presence by observing its effects in your life and relationships now. Identifying that wound honestly is the first step in the healing process that will set you free.

Once we honestly identify our father wound, at whatever level it may exist, we're then faced with the challenge of embracing it.

19 The Healing Process – Step #2: Embracing a Father Wound

THE DIFFERENCE BETWEEN identifying a father wound and embracing it is similar to the difference between watching *SportsCenter* in the comfort of your living room and actually dressing for and preparing to participate in a sport. To identify a father wound means to begin acknowledging it's there, seeing the results in your life and relationships, and beginning to admit honestly to yourself—and likely to another—that it exists in your soul from an inadequate childhood relationship with your father. That crucial first step is an important start.

Embracing that wound is a vital next step beyond this truthful recognition. It's an active welcoming of the wound—a willingness to spend time with it, letting your pain begin to surface so you can feel it after years, perhaps, of denial and fantasy.

Charles Scull proposes, "It seems almost everyone grew up without enough fathering."[68] The more men and women I speak with about their family history and their inner lives, the more I've come to accept the universal nature of Scull's assessment. Yet for many years I felt alone.

Donald Miller is a Christian author who openly reveals his father wound in his compelling books. One reason his books are bestsellers is that he shares his wound in a ruthlessly honest, self-reflective, often raw way. Wounded daughters and sons identify with his story. Miller's dad abandoned him and his sister early in life. He says he didn't even know his father and had no contact with him for nearly thirty years. He honestly wrestles first with identifying and then embracing his wound. His experience paints a picture many of us might relate to. Miller describes his abandonment like this: "You can't blame a kid for feeling unwanted if his father takes off. If you think about it, God gives a father a specific instinct that makes him love his kid more than anything in the world. I suppose that same instinct was floating around in my father's brain, too, but for whatever reason, he took a look at me and split."[69]

Miller goes on to describe in vivid detail the self-deprecating thoughts he lived with due to this abandonment and how crazy it made him feel. He admits to the many negative ways it impacted his life, including an inability to form intimate relationships. He then describes the beginning of his own healing journey, starting with identifying his longing for his father, wishing they had a friendship, and craving his father's affirmation. He writes:

> I don't actually like thinking about this stuff, but I have a sense that wounds don't heal until you feel them. What I mean is, I could lash out against the world for the rest of my life and never stop to do the hard work of asking why I am angry or why I feel pain, then come to the difficult truth that the pain is there because I wanted to be loved, and I wasn't. I wanted to be important to my father, but I wasn't. I wanted to be guided, but I wasn't.

And then honestly, to feel whatever it is that hard truth creates—to respond in the way I needed to respond.[70]

Miller provides a stirring description of identifying and beginning to embrace a father wound. It means allowing the buried pain to rise to the surface of your present experience and feelings. It means no more justifying or making excuses for or blaming others for the way your wound has manifested in your life. It means owning it and taking full responsibility for your life.

When I embraced the truth about my dad and what our relationship must have meant—and not meant—to him, I lost my father in a more profound way. He had removed himself from my life physically many years prior. I now had to give up the fantasy I had clung to of a dad who loved me and felt proud of me—a dad who wanted to be with me and would have been if circumstances were different. No wonder I didn't want to identify and embrace that reality. It hurt like hell.

Truth feels that way sometimes. But it's truth, even painful truth, that ultimately sets us free. Denial keeps our pain locked in the darkness within us.

I reluctantly embraced the distressing truth of who my dad had become and that the sadness I felt was real. That is, I honestly admitted it. Then I had to hold onto that reality as truth and just live with it—not try to make it go away, distract myself from it, project it onto someone else, or alleviate it in an unhealthy or addictive way. Sometimes I succeeded; many times, particularly at first, I did not.

An Inward Look

- ▸ Charles Scull proposes, "It seems almost everyone grew up without enough fathering." Is this statement true for you? Did you grow up without enough fathering?
- ▸ Are there any difficult or painful truths you've identified regarding your relationship with your father? If so, write

them down. You'll need this list to take this "Inward Look" in the next several chapters.

- ▸ Take a look at each one carefully. How successful are you at embracing those truths? That is, are you able to feel the feelings those truths create? Or do you, like I did for so long, tend to ignore those feelings, blame them on someone else, or numb them with some activity or substance?

- ▸ Be as honest as possible about this crucial step. Admitting where we numb our pain, how we blame others, and how we use activities and substances to escape feeling feelings we don't want to feel is critical to embracing our father wound. If we can't do this honestly, we won't move forward toward healing and freedom.

Embracing what was real and not real with
my dad felt depressing—for a long time.
Things got worse before they started
to get better. I started to grieve.

---

20 The Healing Process – Step #3: Grieving a Father Wound

G RIEF IS A COMPLEX emotion and experience. It is not something we normally feel just once. In many ways, grief is like the proverbial onion layers that need to be stripped back over time, one at a time. As in peeling a real onion, working through layers of grief may produce tears, even for us men.

I'm thankful grief is a process and not an event. Removing all the layers at once would be overwhelming. We can handle grief only one wave at a time. Slowly peeling away layers of grief makes for a lengthy process, but it's typically the only way we can manage and heal from it.

I began grieving my father wound in 1991 when I turned thirty. I'm now fifty-two. It would be nice to write about the perfect healing I've achieved, but you'd correctly suspect my lie. I'm not completely through grieving because I still hunger for a father I never had and never will.

I'm still moved to tears during movies and songs about fathers and sons, even about coaches who care about their young athletes and invest in them. My heart still aches at times, even during some of the most joyful moments with my sons, when I consider how different their experience is from mine as a boy. I still feel a hunger to be affirmed, to know that those whom I love approve of me and are proud of me. I still feel insecure around successful and accomplished people. I wonder if I'm okay, if I can make a valuable contribution, and if I'm good enough.

Grief is complex and long lasting, but it does diminish over time when—and only when—one allows grief to be present and to run its course.

The only way to the other side of grief is through it.

We can never circumvent grief, no matter how hard or how long we try. It eventually becomes exhausting to attempt to do so.

We must feel our grief in order to heal it.

I was thirty when I began to face the reservoir of grief in my life. I was terrified of being overwhelmed and consumed by it. When I began to grieve, I started to identify some of the false beliefs I had developed—beliefs I assumed to be true: that there was something mysterious and awfully wrong with me, that I would never get what I wanted, and that I didn't deserve to be happy. As grief gradually ran its course, over a course of years, I started to believe, for the first time in my life, that it was okay for me to be happy, that I did deserve to experience joy as much as anyone else, that there wasn't anything mysteriously flawed about me, and that I could experience the love I longed for.

I was healing. Denial was dying a slow death. I had identified and embraced my father wound and the manifestations of it in my life and relationships. I became more honest with myself and with others.

Healing led me to more truth about my history—my own and my dad's. For the first time, my future looked like something I wanted to live into. I started to grow up inside. It takes a man to be a devoted husband and a great dad. Boys are not equipped yet to fulfill a man's responsibilities.[71] I was finally becoming a man.

Ken Canfield's sage counsel finally made sense to me: "Healing can only occur to the extent that the loss and pain can be described. Basically, I am asking you to find the courage to 'live with the loss,' to live with the ambiguity of a relationship with your father that wasn't all you wanted it to be—to finally admit that some dreams die, and they die hard. You need to grieve."[72]

Even if you've experienced a lesser wound than I've had, you still may need some healing. If so, you must honestly identify your father wound, at whatever depth it exists, then courageously embrace it and slowly grieve. Once you do, you will begin to heal at whatever level you need to.

An Inward Look

- ► Take another look at the list you created at the end of the last chapter identifying areas of inadequacy in your relationship with your dad. Do any of these still cause you pain? Do they still hurt?
- ► Pain must run its course within us if we will ever heal from it. We cannot successfully ignore or deny it, nor can we fully numb it over the long haul of our lives. Eventually, internal pain leaks into our present activities and relationships and causes problems.
- ► Grieving our losses and pain is the only truly effective solution to this problem.

▸ If you are willing to grieve painful losses in your relationship with your dad, I strongly suggest getting some help to do so. I saw several counselors over many years to help me feel and work through my grief.

▸ I also intentionally watched movies that I knew would touch my pain and bring it to the surface. This was scary for me at first, but once I was convinced grieving was good for me, I took this step in small doses as I trusted myself more to handle the feelings.

▸ When feelings came, I slowly learned not to fear them, but to embrace them. That is, I learned to let myself be sad, or cry, or feel the feelings of abandonment, lack of love, or worthlessness I experienced. I slowly became successful at not ignoring, denying, or numbing them. You can do this too.

21 The Healing Process — Step #4: Forgiving Our Fathers

FORGIVING OUR FATHERS is a significant step in the healing journey—forgiving our fathers for what they did or failed to do, for not being all we needed and wanted them to be. Many men try to forgive their fathers too soon, particularly in religious settings, before they have clearly identified their own wound, and before they have honestly embraced it and courageously grieved. In many cases, men discover that such forgiveness is shallow and ultimately ineffective.

Deep and healing forgiveness is best extended *after* a man has worked through a process of identifying and embracing his wound, and then grieving. Real forgiveness means letting go of the resentment, the anger, the fantasy, and, most importantly, the expectation that Dad will ever change or make things right. It also means letting go of one's sense of entitlement to one's anger and resentment or of one's quest to get his needs met in some other, sometimes unhealthy or demanding, way, from something or someone else—particularly a woman.

Real forgiveness requires accepting reality.

Charles Scull writes, "At the heart of our inability to mourn lies a denial of our losses. Our grief helps us to clear the way for more generous feelings toward our fathers. Forgiveness is born in a spirit of generosity. When our cup is full enough, we are able to give something away. At the same time, we receive much when we offer the gift of giving. There is a circularity to forgiveness."[73] This gift of giving contributes to and enriches the act of forgiveness.

Forgiving our fathers does mean letting go of holding them accountable and expecting them to make it right—but that's not all. It also involves our awareness of how we still seek to get needs met that our fathers may not have fulfilled.

Forgiveness and healing include the recognition that we have tried to meet our needs through manipulating people or demanding they make up for what we feel we missed. Forgiveness, therefore, includes letting go of this sort of manipulation and demanding.

Letting go requires that we learn to live with unmet needs.

This is what best-selling psychiatrist Scott Peck referred to as *The Road Less Traveled* in his book by that name. Few people seem willing to pursue their healing journey, and even fewer stay on the path long enough to benefit from it. Because the path to healing is painful and hard, especially initially, and because healing can typically take a long time, often years, many people give up before they find freedom, wholeness, and the quality of life and relationships they long for. For those who stay at it, there is ample reward.

I discovered in my journey toward forgiving my father that he was not a bad man as much as he was a wounded man with his own pain.

I got hurt as a child by the ways that he did and did not deal with his own wounds. As an adult who pursued my own healing, I've accepted that the father wound I experienced as a boy was not something my dad intended. Though it was real, it was not from malice.

Realizing this, I've been able to choose to let the pain go, forgive my dad, and release him, even while he was alive, from my expectation and hope that he would somehow change, make things right, and restore the relationship with him I longed for all my life. I became more able to identify when I was projecting that need onto others and demanding they make up for all my unmet needs.

Family therapist Frank Pittman helped me understand my father better through his writing about his own father. Pittman wrote the following in 1988. He was likely about the same age as my father, slightly younger (my dad was born in 1932). In an article titled "Bringing Up Father," Pittman writes of a time, the 1940s and 1950s, when many of our fathers were growing up. Pittman's insight gave me understanding of what many of our fathers experienced—and possibly lacked. With understanding, I felt more empathy, and it became easier for me to forgive.

How did your dad grow up? What did he experience? Might your father have written something like this?

> Even though I knew I wanted to be a father when I grew up, I didn't know exactly what skills were required. I needed a model of a father, a real live one who could talk to me about what the profession was really like, and how it might differ from my mother's fantasies (and remembrances of her own father). That should not have been too difficult a job. My mother had thoughtfully provided me with a fine father, and it would seem natural for me to have talked to him. But that wasn't the way it worked out—for me, for my friends, or for just about any other man growing up in my generation.

> We of the '40s and '50s grew up with fathers who were off at war or at work and who weren't part of the family even when they were at home. We are essentially fatherless. When we had children, we became fatherless fathers. We either had no concept of what fathers were for, or some glorified fantasy of the paternal role. Lost and confused, we waited for somebody to tell us what we were supposed to do. Some of us assumed that our wives knew what fathers were about, forgetting that our wives hadn't had fathers either.[74]

An essential part of becoming the father you want to be includes resolving any wound in your soul left from your dad that would limit you or prevent you from giving all you desire to give and be all you want to be for your children today. Understanding your father's limitations and forgiving him will help set you free to give to your kids the gift of a more whole and happy dad who is learning to love your children the way they need and crave. In so doing, you'll find further healing yourself.

Real-Life Example

Patrick McMillan is the founder of Teaching Happiness (www .teachinghappiness.com) and the author of *An Exercise in Happiness for Kids*. He is also my friend. He is originally from Canada. Today, Patrick is a great single dad to two boys he adores. Patrick shared with me the very difficult and painful relationship he had with his own father and the challenging forgiveness process he experienced before his father died. I asked if he would be willing to tell his story in this book to give us a picture of how forgiving our fathers can heal and free us. I share the following with Patrick's permission.

> When Keith asked me to write about my experience of forgiving my father, I thought it would be an easy task because, after all, I had already done it. I forgave him

many years ago. How hard could it be to just explain my forgiveness experience in writing?

Well, it turned out to be much more of a challenge than I had first thought it would be. The act of writing has resurfaced many emotions and also a realization that the effect my father had on who I turned out to be was much deeper and had a more profound impact on my life than I had recognized. Most importantly, I experienced, after forgiving my father again at a deeper level, how I was able to transform a relationship I once believed to be adverse and destructive into a positive and constructive experience that altered the rest of my life, especially who I became as a dad.

Although it's very hard for any young boy to believe "my daddy doesn't love me," as I grew older, I just learned to accept it. That realization grew into a deep hatred toward my father for being the worst kind of bully I could imagine. He made bullies at school seem like sissies in comparison. I thought I would never be able to forgive him for telling me and making me believe I was a worthless failure who would amount to nothing and for his brutal physical punishment that went on for many years.

I had to demand he not attend my soccer games because he would embarrass me when he would scream at me from the sidelines and on the way home in the car. As a result of the way my dad spoke to me and treated me, I came to believe I didn't deserve the good things life has to offer. My self-esteem plummeted when he teased me for having ears that stuck out more than other people's.

What I found very troubling was how my father's behavior outside of our home, and the opinion others had of him, was wonderful. Everyone who knew him liked him. He always seemed happy, and others had nothing but great things to say about him. I was told on many occasions as a young boy how lucky I was to have such a great guy for a dad. This made me very angry.

Before completing ninth grade, I couldn't take the bullying any longer. At fifteen years old, with my life's savings of seven dollars, I left home and never went back.

Though I did manage to finish high school while living with friends and their families, and despite going on to the university, I still felt a huge emptiness inside. This empty feeling was my longing to be loved by my father and for him to be proud of me, while understandably hating him at the same time. I believe my empty feeling also came from my firm belief that I would either never become a father or, if I did, I would be far from a good one because I would be like my dad to my own kids. That frightened me. I felt paralyzed. This empty space inside me was a dark and painful place and, unfortunately, one I often visited.

At twenty-nine years old, I realized I was actually in love with the girl who married me so I could get my green card, allowing me to stay in the United States. That realization, coupled with the reality that she did not love me, landed me in that familiar, painful place again.

I knew I had to do something. I had to face my deepest fear that my father didn't love me.

My dad was 2,000 miles away in a nursing home in Canada. I was convinced the hunger inside me—the longing for his love and acceptance—could never be satisfied. It took quite some time for me to get to a place of understanding the meaning and remarkable power of forgiveness. It was not until I tried to really understand my father and feel compassion for him and his life that I began to feel the strength and power I had within me to forgive him.

I learned of the horrific treatment my father endured as a young boy himself by his stepfather after his dad died and his mother remarried when he was only six or seven years old. My dad was eventually pushed out of his house at thirteen years old. Some would ask how a young teenager could make it on the street by himself. The truth is it happens to more kids than you may ever imagine. Like my dad, I was one of them. Many of us do make it, but we live with deep wounds that subconsciously haunt us the rest of our lives. I now realize this was the case with my father. He was never given the tools or support to heal those wounds from his childhood. As unhealed people are prone to do, he subconsciously repeated the life he endured, abusing my brother and me.

I knew I needed to break that destructive cycle. My first step was to feel true empathy, compassion, and understanding toward my father. I booked a flight to Canada to pay him a visit. He had been moved to a hospice before I arrived. He would be made comfortable and be nourished until he died. Knowing this, I wanted to ensure that my visit would provide him peace and comfort.

Regardless of the past, I was grateful to him for bringing me into the world and for all he did to provide for me. I wanted him to know that I loved him. I told him, "I am a dad now myself." We had our first boy who was three at the time and our second who was only a year old. I told my dad, "I am devoting my life to being the best dad I can be to my boys, and I am doing so in your honor. I love you."

He whispered back, "I love you too."

I made peace with and forgave him that day. He passed away less than six months later. He passed knowing I loved and forgave him. When I was told of his passing, my emotions were an odd, though peaceful mix of sadness and joy. They seemed to cancel each other out because I felt almost nothing. I had truly let go of the anger, hatred, and bitterness. I was finally free. The void I once felt in my heart was ultimately filled by dedicating myself to be the father I want to be and by cherishing the opportunity to see my boys grow up to be loving and caring fathers themselves one day.

After finally forgiving my father and after his passing, I felt the energy of his spirit envelop me with love and pride. I now know he did love me in the only way he knew how and that he will always be with me. This is how forgiving my father filled the void in my heart and healed my father wound.

An Inward Look

- ▸ Understanding your father's limitations and forgiving him will help set you free to give to your kids the gift of a more whole and happy dad. What do you know about your father's childhood? What was his relationship with his father like? What limitations did your father possess as a result? If you don't already know, is there anyone you can ask? How can you get more information about your dad and the way he grew up?

▸ Take another look at the list you created identifying areas of inadequacy in your relationship with your dad. This list may provide the things for which you need to forgive your father. Take a careful look now and see if anything else needs to be added. If so, add to your list.

▸ Forgiveness, ultimately, is a letting go. Real forgiveness means letting go of the resentment, the anger, the fantasy, and, most importantly, the expectation that Dad will ever change or make things right. Are you ready to forgive your father?

▸ If not, what are you holding on to? What needs to happen for you to forgive? Write that down.

▸ If you are ready to forgive, here is a sample forgiveness statement you can use (or change this one to fit you, or make up your own). Take each thing you have to forgive your father for and insert your own description of it in this statement: "Dad, when you _____, it wounded me. I am now ready to forgive you for _____. I choose to let go of my anger and resentment of you for _____. And I no longer expect you to make it right. I will live with the consequences of you _____. I forgive you, Dad. I will no longer hold _____ against you.

▸ Read through Patrick's description again of his forgiveness process with his father. As you do, think about what experience you want to create for forgiving your father. Are you ready to make a plan to do so? What action steps do you need to take?

22 The Healing Process — Step #5: Loving Our Children and Healing Ourselves

"Men who are willing to revisit their father hunger can most readily heal themselves by connecting with a child or children."
— Gail Sheehy[75]

O F MY THREE BOYS, my oldest, JD, is most like me in temperament. More than once I've experienced a bit of a time warp, looking at JD while thinking I'm observing myself as a teenager. I often wonder what would happen to his tender heart if I abandoned my family the way my dad left ours. *If I was not a regular presence in his life, how might JD experience that loss? What would it do to him?*

I think I know. Imagining the wound I'd cause in his soul helps me understand my own wound better. Loving JD and staying engaged with him (and both my other boys as well) has actually promoted more healing in me. I've proven to myself that something I've been afraid of all my life isn't true—I'm not just like my father. I can and have made different choices.

My father's life is not my destiny. Nor is your father's life yours.

I feel proud of myself for making my devotion real—to my boys and to myself. It has helped heal part of my father wound. That's very hard to explain. I stay with myself as a boy in my imagination when I stay with my boys in real life. I remain present and engaged with myself as a teenager when I stay with JD. I see myself in him, and I consciously allow myself to love the frightened and sad teenage boy inside of me as I love JD.

When we give to our kids the love we longed for as children, a deep healing takes place because love directed outward is a profound mechanism for promoting inward healing.[76]

As we love another, we heal ourselves.

Your children deserve a father's engaged and loving presence. They benefit, and so do you. I feel it happening in myself. As I give my children the affirmation, acceptance, and affection they long to receive, I heal my own wounds and thus become a better father—more capable of giving more love. You can too. You can love your children, even if you didn't receive that love from your own father, and even if you are no longer married to their mother. Leaving a marriage does not have to mean leaving your children. Stay present; stay engaged. As you do, you'll grow, heal, and become a better, more loving dad.

An Inward Look

- ▶ As we love another, we heal ourselves. Is the idea of loving the boy or teenager inside of you a new concept to you? If so, can you imagine this?
- ▶ You can love your children, even if you didn't receive that love from your own father. And this will be healing for you. Be conscious next time you are sharing affirmation, acceptance, and affection with your children that you may need those same things too. You can give them to yourself now.

23 The Healing Process – Step #6: Fathering Ourselves

LOVING YOUR CHILDREN IS, perhaps surprisingly, part of learning to be a good father to yourself. In being the father to your children they need, you become the father you wish you'd had. You are then able to actually father yourself in ways you wanted and needed to be fathered by your dad.

I am well aware I am not only addressing my sons when I give myself to my boys; when I pay attention and listen to them; when I play with and read to them; when I attend their sporting events and cheer for them and praise them afterwards. I now realize that when I hold them, kiss them, and tell them how much I love them, and when I say to them how lucky and proud I am to be their dad and that I will never neglect or abandon them, I'm also speaking to the little boy and teenager in me who still longs to hear those things from my dad.

In some mysterious way, I'm fathering myself at the same time I'm fathering my sons. As I love my sons, and as I become the great dad for them I wish my dad could have been for me, I continue to heal my own father wound. I can give myself some of the love I'm learning to give my children.

What a gift to our daughters and sons and to us dads as we father, giving to our children what we may not have fully received. We can do this.

For me, this has meant embracing the parts of me that feel incomplete, not affirmed, unloved, and criticized—while at the same time completing myself, affirming myself, accepting myself, loving myself, and being open to how others can do the same for me without demanding that they do so.[77] It means that I've had to stop putting myself down for not being enough and for feeling so incomplete.

Instead, I've chosen to see myself, treat myself, and speak to myself the same way I love my sons. I tell myself I'm now a grown man, I'm now the dad, and I have four sons to nurture and build up, not just the three I produced. There's a fourth son living in my soul who needs a dad to love, affirm, approve of, and accept him. And it's now my job to do that for him—for me.

I'm not as good at loving, affirming, and accepting myself as I am at doing so for my boys, but I'm learning—yes, still learning. I may be a great-grandfather by the time I fully embrace fathering myself, but I'm on the right path now. I'm thankful I'm learning how to be a great dad to my boys—and to myself.

Real-Life Example

A few years ago, on Father's Day, I wrote a few notes of affirmation to several of my friends who were dads early in the morning and sent them off via email to encourage them in their fathering. It occurred to me how much I longed to have my dad tell me what a great dad I had become, that I was loving my boys well, and that my devotion to them was admirable. I decided to write that letter to myself, to be the dad I wish I'd had and father myself the way I would write to and affirm my own sons. I did it. And though at first it did seem a bit odd and awkward, by the second paragraph it felt great. Another level of healing took place that day.

The more I love my sons and the more honest I am about the wounded boy in me, the better I become at fathering me too. It's actually working. I'm learning to heal myself. I'm happier and more aware of how much of me there is now to give away to others, such as the dads I coach. (You can learn more about personal Great Dad Coaching at www.thegreatdadsproject.org/resources/coaching).

Fathering yourself is part of your ongoing healing. And it helps you be a better dad to your children.

An Inward Look

▸ Does the boy or teenager inside you need some good fathering?

▸ Consider writing yourself your own Great Dad Tribute as I did for myself on Father's Day a few years ago. You don't have to wait for Father's Day. You can affirm yourself any time. Doing so is a remarkably healing experience. Try it. Give to yourself the affirmation you'd love to hear your own dad give you.

24   A Power Greater Than Ourselves

PART OF THE GENIUS of the twelve-step programs is the dual recognition they've built into the very first step toward sobriety. To even begin the program, an individual must admit that he is powerless over his addiction and must declare his need for and dependence upon a power greater than himself to help him change. The same is true in the healing journey I've described and embraced myself.

Alcoholics Anonymous (AA) provides a useful model for inclusive language regarding personal transformation and spiritual awareness. Their terminology of a *higher power* has allowed millions of recovering alcoholics from vastly diverse walks of life to embrace in a supportive, worldwide community a concept of God as each person understands him. God is thus a higher power who provides the spiritual presence and strength to transform the alcoholic's mind and behavior and to break the addictive cycle so the addict can become permanently sober.

In my own healing journey and in the recovery of thousands, I have experienced and witnessed the need for a higher power—beyond our self-limited experience. The success of the AA model demonstrates it doesn't actually matter how people conceive of this higher power or what they call it; surrendering to God as one understands him and reaching out for help from God works. It is powerfully effective to the point of being essential.

During the most intense years of my healing experience, I conceived of God as the Jewish and Christian tradition describes him, as a loving father. (I use a masculine reference here for convenience, not to support a view of God as male). By embracing God as a father, I slowly substituted in my mind the image and experience I came to have of God for the experience I had with my father. As I conceived it, through years of transforming healing, the love of a father in heaven slowly replaced and healed the pain I endured with my father on earth.

By projecting my hunger for a father's love and my need for his affirmation and acceptance onto God, I applied the steps I described in this section of the book, "Healing a Father Wound." I believed that God was for me, that he unconditionally loved me, and that he did not see me as mysteriously flawed. I believed that he accepted me, and that I belonged in his family.

All of these beliefs and others like them, allowed me—in fact, compelled me—to eventually accept and love myself. These spiritual beliefs helped me let go of my long-held false beliefs and the pain they produced—pain I endured and embraced as a child. My belief in a power greater than myself and the process of choosing to replace my old, false beliefs with these spiritual beliefs ultimately enabled me not only to *accept* myself but also later to *father* myself.

Whether we adhere to a theistic system such as Judaism, Christianity, or Islam, embrace nontheistic universal laws of humanity, or believe in some other personal way, as we let go of ourselves to God as we conceive him and reach out for his love and power, we invite and promote the healing we may need.

25 Conclusion: Healing a Father Wound

To one degree or another, all of our fathers were imperfect; even the very best dads made mistakes. That's just part of being human. Few of our fathers had good models or training for what it means to be a great dad. There doesn't need to be anything shocking or dismaying about that. It just is what it is. And when you became a dad, you joined the swelling membership of the Well-Intentioned-But-Imperfect-Dads Club. Welcome. Take any empty seat—if you can find one.

Recognizing and admitting our own imperfections is humbling, but it can also lead us to reach out for help—for wisdom from those who have gone before and made some progress. The unwelcome reality is that we will wound our daughters and sons on some level even though we may be careful not to do so.

Real-Life Example

One of my friends I consider a great dad shared with me the way he wounded his son and his daughter when they became teenagers. He didn't handle their natural separating well during those turbulent years. On several occasions, he forced his way into their lives when they were clearly saying they didn't want to talk about something and he overstepped boundaries he should have respected, such as going into his daughter's room and looking through some of her mail. He unwittingly communicated he didn't trust his kids to make wise choices and he didn't believe they were capable to make it on their own. It angered and hurt his kids. It created distance between him and both of them.

My friend shared with me that when he came to realize years later the mistakes he made, he sought and achieved a meaningful resolution with both of his children. He acknowledged his mistakes, shared his regrets, and apologized. Both his grown son and his adult daughter forgave him, shared their own regrets, and affirmed their love for him.

Pay Close Attention to Your Inner Life

One of the most important, though often ignored practices of becoming a great dad is paying close attention to your own inner life, especially identifying and embracing your father wound. That wound will limit your effectiveness as a dad and your ability to enjoy your fathering and your children.

We will experience substantial healing as we grieve—as much and as long as our wound requires. As we learn more about our dads and about ourselves, we will grow in compassion for our fathers as well as empathy toward ourselves, and we can choose to forgive. Genuine forgiveness lets go of the anger, the resentment, the need for our dads to make it right, as well as the demand that our unfulfilled needs be met in some other way or by some other person. And we finally begin to feel free—free to fully engage with and to freely give to our children; free to immensely enjoy them; free not to repeat our father's mistakes. Your father's life is not your destiny.

My own journey was proof enough for me that the considerable healing of a father wound is an indispensible element of good fathering. If a wound exists, it must be substantially healed. To the extent it is healed, the greater our chances of becoming the great dads we desire to be. Healing brings freedom, freedom leads to love, and love produces relationships that last a lifetime and create joy, laughter, and meaning.[78]

There's So Much More to Say

There is much more I want and need to say and more you will experience in your own journey of healing, particularly in terms of seeking a new relationship with your dad, reconnecting with him, even reconciling with him if the relationship is broken and if your dad is still alive.[79] More needs to be said to men whose fathers are no longer living, nor available for one reason or another, and to those whose fathers continue to reject and wound. I understand this. For now, I hope that what I've shared will point you in the right direction.

If nothing more, I hope these chapters increase your awareness of the power you have as a father to shape your sons and daughters—how your words and actions profoundly affect them and make lifelong impressions. I also hope it makes you cognizant of the ways you might unintentionally wound the children you love.

Our sons need to know we approve of them and are proud of them. Let's tell them and show them the love and approval they crave. In countless ways over many years, we need to communicate our unconditional and unending acceptance.

Our daughters need to know that we feel attached to them and that we accept them, are proud of them, and love them just as they are. Let's tell them how capable, smart, and beautiful they are and show them we believe they can accomplish anything they desire and become whomever they want to be.

We will minimize any wound we might inadvertently create in our kids by affirming, accepting, and loving them as deeply and fully as we are able. We need to honestly and humbly apologize when we come short of our goal—which we will, because we all do. Our own healing will enable and energize us to do so in more free and meaningful ways. Perhaps more than any of the other fathering practices I could suggest, our healing will free us to become great dads—the effective and fulfilled fathers we want to be.

For dads who have children with whom you feel you have made significant, even perhaps irreparable mistakes, may this teaching encourage you as to how much your children are likely still longing to reconcile with you and to receive your affirmation, acceptance, and affection.

Take the first step. Believe that you still can and will be the dad you hope to be and your children need you to be. Even if the wound you created is deep and painful, you still have power to affirm and heal. Your children hunger for you, even if they don't quite know how to articulate that hunger. You will meet a profound need and begin a healing process that you both need.

Part III

Taking Action

"What is important is to just get started.
Get into the game. Get on the playing field.
Once you do, you will start to get feedback that
will help you make the corrections you need to
make to be successful. Once you are in action, you
will start learning at a much more rapid rate."

Jack Canfield, *The Success Principles*

26 It Takes More Than Desire

It is one thing to study war and another to live the warrior's life.
—Telemon of Arcadia,
mercenary of the fifth-century B.C.E.

H AVE ONE OF YOUR KIDS ever asked you a question you didn't know how to answer? When my oldest son, JD, was only a first grader, he stunned me with this: "Dad, why did your dad leave your family?"

We were playing chess on the floor while away for a few days at a mountain cabin. JD and Cal were with me; Kai was home with Mom. Nothing we were saying or doing could have prompted his question. My mind raced. *Why would JD ask this? Why now? What can I say that would be honest but appropriate? How honest should I be?* I searched JD's inquisitive eyes. He seemed sad. I stalled, "Well, let's see, um. . . ."

My boys knew that my parents divorced when I was young and that I didn't grow up with my dad nearly as much as I wanted. Because we had talked about these things in general, age-appropriate ways, they knew I missed having a father who loved me and stayed with me.

Five years after my dad disappeared from our lives, JD was asking me why my dad left my family when I was a boy. How would I answer this difficult question? I fumbled this reply: "JD, my dad didn't know how to be in a family. He wasn't happy, and I don't think he wanted to be the kind of husband and father a man needs to be to commit to a family. So, he left to do what he thought would make him happy."

JD stared at me. He tilted his head to one side as if trying to find a place in his brain for my unsatisfying answer. JD responded quietly, "Okay." And we continued playing chess. I thought that was the end of that conversation.

The next day we played in the snow. We rode sleds and had a raucous snowball fight. Cal and JD, then five and almost seven, formed a formidable offense and attacked me repeatedly, without mercy, from all directions. I was a willing target and dramatic victim. We retreated to the cozy cabin, took off our cold, wet gear, and warmed ourselves by the fire with some hot chocolate. JD grew quiet, then looked at me and asked, "Dad, why did your dad leave your family?"

Why is he asking me again? I tried to answer in a clearer way: "JD, I don't think my dad thought much about how his words or actions might hurt other people, including his family. So when my dad decided he didn't want to be married or be a full-time dad anymore, he left our family to live his own life."

I didn't feel great about that answer either. It was honest, but it hardly made sense to me at forty-four. What could it mean to my nearly seven-year-old son? JD again stared at me. He appeared distant and confused. "Okay," he said.

The third day we had a pillow fight in the morning that led to a full-on wrestling match. We laughed and ran all over the cabin, imitating big-time wrestlers—flexing our muscles, grunting, and growling. I was called for using illegal tickle tactics. When it was time to leave, we cleaned the cabin and packed the car. We ate our peanut butter and jelly sandwiches and began our trip down the mountain toward home.

About thirty quiet minutes later, JD leaned forward as much as he could stretch and put his head between the two front seats. A third time he asked, "Dad, why did your dad leave your family?"

JD was obsessing over this painful reality of my life, but I had no idea why. I needed a different approach. I reached my hand back to hold his, looked into his eyes in the rear view mirror, and said, "JD, I just don't think my dad understood how much I needed him."

My son sat back with a troubled, distant look. He timidly said, "Okay."

We drove in silence for what seemed like ten minutes, though it must have been just a moment. JD leaned forward between the front seats again and with a soft, unsteady voice asked, "Dad, you know how much I need you?"

Oh, my. This must have been the question my son was trying to ask and had been brooding over for days. He was scared. He knew that my dad left my family when I was seven years old. JD was now a couple of weeks from that same birthday. And though I'm sure I had never given him reason to think so, in his mind he must have concluded that boys lose their dads when they turn seven—that's when dads leave.

In my previous answers I provided *information*. What JD craved was *affirmation*. He needed me to assure him that I was his dad, he was my son, I loved him, and that would never change.

I said, "My boys, I will never abandon or forsake you. I love you. And I will be your dad as long as I live."

There were no fireworks or grand recognitions of my resolute daddy speech—no award given for my enduring commitment and devotion. JD smiled, leaned back in his seat with a noticeable sigh, and said, "Good."

He's never asked again.

A Transformation of Identity Begins

That was a life-defining moment in my development as a dad. That weekend, I absorbed what I thought I already knew—how much I matter to my boys, how much every dad matters to his kids, how much you matter to yours.

For the rest of the ride home, my heart was full with love for my boys. I reveled in the value I felt as their dad. I still don't know why it didn't matter more to my father to be a dad to me and to my brother. What I do know is that it matters to me. Although I already desired to be a good dad, on that drive home, I let that defining moment sink in. It slowly transformed how I perceived my identity. I dedicated myself to the awesome responsibility, privilege, and joy of becoming a great dad—whatever that took. I felt as if I would never be the same again. I believed that moment of insight and inspiration would transform me forever.

Have you ever experienced an epiphany of insight or a profound feeling of inspiration that you thought would transform your life forever, that you would never again be the same?

What I found, to my great disappointment, was that that moment of profound inspiration and dedication to something new was just that, a moment. Life-change didn't magically happen. I did not mysteriously become what I longed now to be. It took work—years of it—and thoughtful, premeditated effort to actually grow, change, heal, and become the dad I wanted to be.

I had to get a vision in my mind of what being a great dad actually would look like for me and then make the challenging life- and career-adjusting decisions to foster the change I had hoped might somehow miraculously occur. It didn't. I had to make it happen. My strong desire wasn't enough. I soon learned that transformation takes more than desire.

27 How Change Happens

Six frogs sat on a lily pad.
One decided to jump off.
How many are left?

Most people answer "five." Isn't it obvious? Of the six frogs sitting on the pad, only one made a decision to jump. Six minus one equals five, right? Well, if this were a simple math problem, five would be the correct answer. But this is a riddle that captures one of the counterintuitive mysteries of human psychology and behavior. The conundrum might at first be represented mathematically by this equation.

Decision = Action = Results

Many people believe this is how the sequence works. First, we have a strong desire that leads us to make a conscious decision to do something—to change in some way. Then we naturally take actions that produce the results our decision intended. But does this work? Is this what we see in reality?

Do you know anyone who decided to stop smoking but is still smoking?

Do you know anyone who decided to lose weight but still needs to?

Do you know anyone who decided to make more money but hasn't?

Do you know anyone who decided to improve his marriage but . . .

Though that equation appears rational, it is not automatic; in many cases, it just doesn't represent reality. The hard truth is that making a decision does not necessarily mean much. It does not inevitably produce action that leads to the outcomes we hope for or intend.

> Six frogs sat on a lily pad.
> One decided to jump off.
> How many are left?

The surprising answer to the riddle is "six." There are still six frogs sitting on that safe lily pad because although one *decided* to jump, he never actually jumped. He resolved to change his location, but he didn't. He never followed through on the decision he made to change. So he's still sitting there with his mates, knowing he should jump but sitting rather still.

The Decision = Action = Results equation doesn't actually represent the way we change. Transformation of behavior, and therefore the accomplishment of our goals and desires, doesn't happen that way. There needs to be a slight and apparently subtle change to the equation, but in reality, it's a profound adjustment. It's an adjustment that leads to change—that causes the critical shift from information to transformation. It's how our decisions to change stick, producing the change we intend.[80] See whether you notice the slight but significant modification to the equation below.

Decision + Action = Results

Did you catch it? It's such a subtle variation on paper—a mere plus sign where an equal sign once existed—but it's a massive shift in reality. In order for our friendly frog to actually get off his safe lily pad and get wet, he has to do more than *want* to move and more than make a decision. His decision needs to be accompanied by action—specific acts consciously made to produce the results his decision anticipates. In short, he needs to follow through on his action plan.

It's only when our frog works out his desire and decision in specific, carefully evaluated, and monitored actions that desired results manifest. It's not magic, but in some ways, it appears magical when it actually happens because it happens too infrequently. Someone once noted that the road to hell is paved with something. Remember? Good intentions! Intentions get us nowhere unless we act on them.

Smokers *can* quit smoking.

Overweight folks *can* lose weight.

People *can* make more money and
improve their marriages.

Fathers *can* become great dads.

After what you've read, I hope you've made the decision to be the best dad you can possibly be. I've provided three specific, crucial fathering skills (affirmation, acceptance, and affection) and pointed you in the direction of healing your father wound to help you achieve your desire. And I've inspired you with stories. You're convinced you want to be a great dad.

Will you be? You will if you actually take the specific steps you need to in order to turn your desire and good decision into specific actions that will produce the results you want and your kids will love.

I've collected all the specific action steps I've shared throughout the book in appendix A.

One More Addition to the Equation

Please indulge me to say one more thing about our Decision + Action = Results equation. It really should be represented this way:

$$Decision + Action + Beliefs = Results$$

The challenge is that our beliefs are mostly nonconscious. If our nonconscious beliefs contradict our desires, decisions, or actions, they will sabotage them and render the results we intend less effective and, in some cases, unattainable. Pursuing an intended result while harboring negative or limiting beliefs is much like attempting to drive a car with the emergency break on. In the section "Healing a Father Wound," I illustrated how that worked in my life for many years.

Though that is a more complex teaching than space here allows to explain, I do want to mention it so you know there is ultimately more to transformation—to becoming the great dads we want to be—than simply making decisions and taking actions.[81] If making good decisions about being a great dad and taking actions that should change you don't help you achieve the progress you hope for or the results you desire, you may need to look more deeply at your subconscious, limiting beliefs. Subconscious beliefs refer to the thinking that was shaped in us through our childhood and young adult experiences, particularly with and by our dads.

Books such as *The Success Principles* by Jack Canfield, *The Happiness Hypothesis* by Jonathan Haidt, and the first half of *The Answer: Grow Any Business, Achieve Financial Freedom, and Live an Extraordinary Life* by John Assaraf and Murray Smith might be a good place to start. One of the best books—for those who are serious about taking a close look at their subconscious beliefs—is Scott Peck's riveting bestseller, *The Road Less Traveled.* Seeing a competent psychologist might be a needed step. The individual and small group Great Dad Coaching I offer also assists dads to identify and resolve subconscious beliefs that inhibit a man from becoming the dad he longs to be. (See www .thegreatdadsproject.org/resources/coaching).

The Elephant and Rider

Jonathan Haidt, a researcher, teacher, and social psychologist at the University of Virginia, performs experiments to figure out what he calls "one corner of human social life." His corner consists of morality and moral emotions. In his thoughtful book, *The Happiness Hypothesis: Finding Modern Truth in Ancient Wisdom*, he proposes a metaphor he has been formulating for ten years. It's a metaphor about how the human mind works and why change is difficult—a rider on an elephant.[82]

The rider, Haidt says, is our conscious, decision-making, rational mind. Given the context of our twenty-first century philosophical culture, he proposes our conscious mind is that with which we most identify. From years of research, Haidt argues that the least influential part of our psyche is our conscious mind. Instead, he posits the elephant, our powerful subconscious, feelings-driven mind, is by far the most decisive in determining how we actually live: "The elephant and the rider each have their own intelligence, and when they work together well they enable the unique brilliance of human beings. But they don't always work together well."[83] In fact, there are many instances when the impulses of the elephant stand in defiant opposition to the reasoning of the rider. In such instances, the elephant goes its own way regardless of the commands the rider might whisper, state, or even shout.

Haidt contends that this is why people keep doing such stupid things, even when they have clearly seen the consequences of their behavior and have decided to change—why people cannot control themselves and continue to do what they know isn't good for them. It's why some fathers who long to be better dads don't actually become them.

The metaphor Haidt developed explains why willpower alone (the rider) rarely creates the positive change many people hope to achieve. It describes the nature of addiction. It also explains why logical arguments about moral issues are often pointless and ineffective. Haidt asks, "When you refute a person's argument, does she generally change her mind and agree with you? Of course not, because the argument you defeated was not the cause of her position; it was made up after the judgment was already made."[84]

The elephant is the one who makes moral judgments, often irrespective of rational logic and argument. Hence, arguments rarely, if ever, effect change in one's feelings that produce moral stances. No father ever got argued or simply inspired into becoming a great dad who wasn't one already, or didn't want to become one.

In an important paragraph of his chapter "Changing Your Mind," Haidt addresses my predicament on my car ride home from the mountain cabin and the weeks and months that followed. If you've ever had an epiphany—a sudden moment of great insight—if you've ever been inspired to change your life and then found that your moment of insight faded and you either never did achieve the change you envisioned or slipped back to your regular routine weeks or months after making some changes, then you're not alone. Psychologists refer to this as regressing; addicts call it relapsing; Haidt demonstrates it's just normal human behavior.

Lasting change doesn't happen that way. Observe Haidt's conclusion after twenty years of research into human social/psychological behavior: "Epiphanies can be life-altering, but most fade in days or weeks. The rider can't just decide to change and then order the elephant to go along with the program. Lasting change can come only by retraining the elephant, and that's hard to do. When pop psychology programs are successful, which they sometimes are, they succeed not because of the initial moment of insight but because they find ways to alter people's behavior over the following months. **They keep people involved with the program long enough to retrain the elephant.**"[85]

My mission, therefore, is to help you stay involved in your own program of change—your growth toward becoming the great dad you want to be—*long enough* so you actually achieve the transformation you seek. If you enjoy this book, I'm thankful, but that's not enough. If you are inspired by it to become a great dad, again I'm grateful, but that's not why I wrote this book. I wrote it with the expectation not only to inspire your rider (your conscious, decision-making center) but also to begin retraining your elephant (your emotional, sub-conscious, automatic mind that most powerfully influences your behavior, your decisions, and your life). I want to do far more for you than pique your interest or inspire your thoughts. My ultimate goal is to help you transform your life and radically improve your relationships with your kids. So this book is just a beginning. In fact, it's an invitation to more.

That's what this last section of the book is about. What specific behaviors do you need to regularly practice to keep your fire burning? Which activities will lead you further down the path of change? What do you need to do every day, each week, and throughout the months and years ahead to become an even better dad than you are right now—to become the great dad you long to be? The next couple of chapters point you in the right direction.

28 Consistent Input and Helpful Practices

THE FIRST THING I invite you to do is to register for The Great Dads Project Community of Dads on our website (www.thegreat dadsproject.org). Thousands of men like you are self-selecting into a vibrant community of fathers who together are moving toward a shared goal. It is my commitment to contribute regular communication including in-depth research, compelling writing, speaking, and leadership to a burgeoning movement of dads who desire greatness in their fathering. So many dads now desire depth, meaning, and fulfilling love and laughter in their relationships with their kids. Become a part of this community with us.

By registering for the Community of Dads, you'll receive directly from me regular communication specifically crafted to inspire, educate, train, and support you. You'll get first access to inspirational messages, educational materials, and live and virtual training events that not only provide a needed skill set but also elevate your spirit to promote bonding with your children. That is, I'll help you create a new mindset. Together, we'll retrain your elephant. As a member of our Community of Dads, you'll also obtain access to individual and small group coaching.

Around the country, I'm creating peak experiences for fathers that stimulate self-awareness, receptivity, and transformation not just by elevating men's conscious minds but also by touching the depth of subconscious emotions that lead to change. Professor of psychology Abraham Maslow, in a small gem of a book *Religions, Values, and Peak-Experiences*, demonstrates that peak experiences—extraordinary, self-transcendent moments that feel very different from ordinary life—flood people with feelings of wonder, awe, joy, love, and gratitude. Such feelings lead to bonding with those with whom we share the peak experience and those whom are closest to us: in our case, our children.

Peak experiences are available to all who will welcome them. Maslow writes: "Our findings indicate that all or almost all people have or can have peak-experiences." Maslow even divides humanity as to the ability to welcome and embrace peak experiences. He calls the two camps "peakers" and "non-peakers." His point is that peak experiences help us grow, heal, and become the dads we long to be.[86]

Regular Helpful Practices

As a member of The Great Dads Project Community of Dads, you'll receive regular input that expands what I share in the following bullet list. The following are practical ideas on how to keep good, inspiring, great dad input flowing your way. These are all steps I take to keep my own father-fire burning. You will find additional resources including reviews and quotes from fathering books placed on our website.

Remember the following suggestions by the first word of each. Use the first letter of each suggestion to spell three trees: a PALM, a FIR, and an OAK.

PALM:

> ▸ **Practice** regularly the action steps listed in appendix A.

▸ **Attend** live and virtual events with other men on fathering. I'll keep you informed about the ones I present and others I support.

▸ **Listen** to inspiring reminders and teaching related to fathering, life transformation, and healing. I do this often while I drive. Get CDs (such as the ones I produce for our Community of Dads, and others), audio messages, podcasts—whatever you can find. I will recommend specific resources for dads to The Community of Dads.

▸ **Meditate** daily on the vision these practices will create in your mind of your best self as a dad. Napoleon Hill, the man Andrew Carnegie commissioned to interview 100 of the world's most successful men and who recorded his observations in his phenomenal bestseller *Think and Grow Rich*, famously asserted, "What the mind can conceive and believe, the mind can achieve." I teach dads how to do this, as I practice it daily myself.

FIR:

▸ **Find** and regularly visit websites such as www.thegreatdads project.org, www.tumblon.com, www.teachinghappiness .com, www.zelawelakids.com, and others, as well as daddy blogs that inspire you toward your goal. See my suggestions on my website under Resources.

▸ **Identify** some potential dad mentors and ask them, one by one, if they will spend some time with you, talk with you about fathering, answer your questions, and help you grow. Get my eBook or audio CD on "Fathering in Community" to learn more about this.

▸ **Read** good books on being a great dad regularly. I help our Community of Dads identify these.

OAK:

> ▸ **Organize** family goals based on a Great Dad Purpose Statement and review them regularly. Get my eBook or audio CD that teaches dads how to do this: "Craft a Great Dad Purpose Statement."
>
> ▸ **Attend** or start a small group with other dads who share your commitment to being the best dad you can be. Get my eBook or audio CD, "Fathering in Community." Then download a sample small group discussion guide from my website (www .thegreatdadsproject.org/resources/smallgroups).
>
> ▸ **Kraft** a Great Dad Purpose Statement, memorize it, and say it daily to yourself every morning during some quiet, reflective, meditative time. Think of creative ways to live your purpose statement each day in some way. I teach dads how to craft their own Great Dad Purpose Statement and why to do so.

Okay, sorry about the K in Kraft. My sons helped me figure this out, and we couldn't come up with any other three-letter name for a tree that used the letter C for Craft. If you absolutely must, you can think about macaroni and cheese for the last suggestion in OAK.

Other than the suggestions above related to the Internet, these are the regular practices I suggested to Bobby Colombo while he was still in prison. The more I visited the prison to teach and coach the men of PEP, the greater Bobby's desire and commitment grew—he really wanted to change. He longed to become the best dad he could be to the two children he left behind nearly six years prior when he was incarcerated. Bobby asked me to coach him, to help him, and to give him the kind of great dad input and encouragement he knew he needed.

I was delighted to do so, particularly when I observed, over time, he was serious. Every book I gave him, he read. Every assignment I asked him to do, he did. When I suggested he begin writing regular, encouraging, affirming letters to his children, he did so with increasing regularity and delight. He wrote letters to me in between my visits, and I always wrote back to him. In June 2009, Bobby wrote me this letter. I share it with his permission just as he wrote it.

Dear Keith,

Most of the time when I write someone involved with PEP that donates their time into helping us, I try to push that little button in their heart and make them feel the same sensation within that I feel when they show that they care.

You are more than just "someone involved with PEP," you are our PEP father. You are a great example of a father which most of us never had. You yourself know how deep and serious a father wound can be and for me, you provide hope that I can stop the cycle now.

I look forward to perpetuating your teaching about fathering. I wish for a day when you hear of how I am doing well as a father. Well at life. And I hope that when you hear that, it will be rewarding for you and all the effort that you put into teaching us. I can only imagine how hard it is to leave your precious children and come be with us. I can never thank you enough for inspiring and encouraging me to be the best father that I can.

Some day soon I will make myself and you proud when I myself become a great father. And from someone with very, very deep father wounds, I wanted to tell you how proud I am of you. I'm proud that you are there for your boys and I am proud that you try to make a way for healing for others, even their children.

Love, Bobby

Action Steps

The most important step from information to transformation is action—taking action on all the good information you've read and on your own strong desire to become the effective and fulfilled father you want to be. With the worthy goal of real transformation in view, I'm going to pull together into one place (appendix A) the practical suggestions and ideas I've provided along the way. I suggest keeping a bookmark at this appendix once you've finished reading the book. By doing so, you can regularly come back to these action steps for inspiration and suggestions for activities you can do with your kids—activities that will help you love and enjoy them, affirm and encourage them, and foster your relationship with them as you build their self-esteem, respect, discipline, and security.

You can also go to our website to download your own copy of these action steps to post in a place you can see and review them regularly. (See www.thegreatdadsproject.org/resources/actionsteps.)

Personal Coaching

Like many athletes or executives who find it helpful to have a professional coach to hone their game or business skills, a growing number of fathers have discovered the benefit of personal coaching to help them become great dads. I've coached many fathers toward their goal of becoming better dads and I thoroughly enjoy the process and results. I love to see dads put into practice the skills we work on together and achieve fathering success—enjoying closer relationships with their kids that make them both happier. I love to see kids get what they need and long for from their dads, and dads find fulfillment in becoming the dads they want to be.

I coached Bobby Colombo for three years. I've shared part of his story already (you'll read Bobby's perspective in the epilogue). When I started coaching Bobby, he hadn't seen his daughter or son for six years. They had almost no relationship. Bobby felt like a failure as a father, though he desired nothing more than to become a good dad. We worked together over a long period of time toward the restoration of relationships with his children.

Today, Bobby is free—from prison but also from regrets. He's a great dad who now enjoys great relationships with his kids. I asked Bobby whether he wanted to share something about our coaching experience with other dads who might be considering a coaching relationship. He said he'd be delighted to and sent me the following:

> Keith Zafren taught me so much about being a dad. He is a great mentor and I love him dearly for what he taught me. Keith coached me for three years. He is an excellent teacher and even better father. He leads by example. I moved forward light years in my fathering skills because of what I learned from Keith. After just a few minutes of his teaching, you'll know that his special calling is to help men become great dads. Allow Keith to mold you into a great dad. I know I am.

If you'd like to explore whether personal great dad coaching might be a good fit for you, contact me through our website (www.thegreatdadsproject.org) for a free consultation. We'll talk about your situation and your goals to see whether coaching would be a good fit for you.

How Do You Stay Focused on Becoming a Great Dad?

1. Get ongoing great dad input (join The Great Dads Project Community of Dads).

2. Apply the regular, helpful practices listed in this chapter (PALM, FIR, OAK).

3. Follow the action steps given in this book (see appendix A).

4. Consider personal coaching.

5. Accept The Great Dad Challenge™ (see the next chapter).

29 The Great Dad Challenge™

WHENEVER I SPEAK TO DADS, I always invite men who are willing to accept a specific challenge I call The Great Dad Challenge™. This challenge is for dads to spend time each day for the next fifteen days with their children, individually, and to affirm them while demonstrating acceptance and showing some affection. For those who express their desire to embrace the challenge by standing and responding with a verbal commitment, I provide a black silicon wristband that has written on it in all capital, white letters THE GREAT DAD CHALLENGE.

I wear mine all the time. I ask dads who accept this challenge to wear their wristband for the duration of time they're living out their commitment to the challenge. Then if they want to keep it on afterward as a reminder, as I do, that's their choice.

Phase 1 of The Great Dad Challenge™ is called "The High Five." Dads accept the challenge to spend five minutes each day with each child for the next five days. For dads who have more than three children, it's fine to focus on three kids at a time. For instance, if a man has five children, focus on three kids for fifteen days, then the other two for fifteen days.

Your task for five minutes is only to listen to whatever your kids want to talk about, without critique or evaluation but with active engagement. Near the end of the five minutes, share a verbal affirmation of your child (each day, for five days), including some form of physical affection while expressing acceptance.

Dads, you can use a phrase such as "I think you're terrific, and I'm so glad you're mine; I'll love you forever, no matter what," or you can create your own. If you miss a day, remove the wristband and transfer it to the other wrist, then start The High Five over. That's right, five more days of listening and affirming with affection and acceptance. If you miss a day again, then start over again. The goal for The High Five is five days in a row without missing a day.

Once successful, that is, once you spend five minutes each day with each child for five consecutive days, affectionately affirming and accepting, take your kids out to celebrate in some way. It can be any size celebration that schedule and finances allow, but do something to mark the accomplishment and the growing relationships.

After this first celebration, you move to phase 2 of the challenge, "The Hang Ten." For the next ten days, spend ten minutes each day with each of your children doing the same thing: listening actively without critique or evaluation, then affirming with affection and acceptance. The same rule about consecutive days is in play. If you miss a day, transfer your wristband to the other wrist and start The Hang Ten over. After successfully completing this second phase of the challenge, go out for a great celebration.

My boys are the ones who added the celebration aspect to the challenge. When I first created this challenge, I told them why I was wearing my GREAT DAD CHALLENGE wristband. They said, "That's pretty cool, Dad, but you need to tell the dads to take their kids out to celebrate when they get it right." They were absolutely right. Go ahead and celebrate.

If you already are a part of some sort of small support group, I encourage you to share in your group before you begin your Great

Dad Challenge experience what you're about to do and why. Then share along the way for encouragement, support, and accountability.

I ask dads, at the end of fifteen days, to report back to their small groups what happened, celebrate with them after the challenge is completed successfully, and post their results to The Great Dads Project site (Community of Dads Forum). You'll find encouraging stories there from other dads about how The Great Dad Challenge™ worked for them and their children.

Real-Life Stories

Here are six real-life examples from dads who attended one of my live seminars, accepted The Great Dad Challenge™, and later wrote to me sharing their experiences. These stories were so moving and inspiring, I asked these dads if I could share their stories publicly. With their permission, here are some regular dads just like us who accepted the challenge and experienced remarkable results—results you and I can achieve as well.

Martin:

I've kept to the challenge most days and I'm finding it to be a lot of fun. It has challenged me to think about what my kids are interested in and to ask them questions about what they like to get them talking. I've also benefitted by taking a step back to assess what each of their strengths and talents are. I try to speak into these areas as I affirm them each night. It's been really good to bond with my kids, especially with Joey (age five) because I tend to be the hardest on him. I've found myself to be more patient with him lately.

Also, the Challenge wristband prompted a discussion with a guy from work today who is a father as well. Gave us each a chance to talk about how important it is to spend time with our kids and not to work so much. Thanks for all the great advice.

Adam:

I realized how often I don't give my children (seven, five, and three years old) quality interaction. I'm traveling this week, so it's a good opportunity to send written affirmations via email.

The most remarkable thing happened the other night while I was having a heart-to-heart talk with my seven-year-old son before leaving on my trip abroad. He was upset to the point of tears, which is uncharacteristic of him. So I laid down next to him on the bed and shared what was in my heart.

I told him how it ached inside when I was a boy and could not be with my father. How now my heart aches when I'm not with him. I told him I loved him very much along with affirmations. He was fine after that, but the most visible change came in the morning when he was peppy and relaxed around me (like you feel when you're fully accepted by someone). This was pleasing to see for I had forgotten how his desire to please me has caused him stress, perhaps for several months. Makes me sad and regretful I caused him stress. The good news is that children are resilient and I caught this now—thanks to your seminar (so thank you).

My five-year-old girl is just eating up the affirmations. I think my three-year-old daughter gets it but she seems too young to give visible clues, except perhaps a calmness that comes over her.

So, you're making a difference!!! Keep up the great work, Keith.

Tony:

I have three kids, a girl, twenty, a son, seventeen, and a son, eight. I started affirming my boys right after the seminar but had a hard time catching up with my daughter. I went to lunch with her last week and sat and listened to her as closely as I could and tried to not interrupt. I remembered part of one of the sayings that you had at the back of the packet.

"As long as I have a penny, you'll never be broke. As long as I have food, you'll never go hungry. As long as I have a roof over my head, you'll never be homeless."

When I spoke this to her, we both cried and I felt a bond that I never felt with my parents begin to grow with my daughter!

Thank you.

Steve:

My experience is that now my children expect me to spend five minutes with them every night and want my affirmation. My eight-year-old daughter said one night, as I was praying over her, "What about my five minutes, Dad?" I have prayed over my children for as long as I can remember at night after tucking them in bed and then I turn the lights out and leave the room. But on this night, she noticed that I skipped the affirmation time including five minutes of talking to and listening to my children. Even my teenagers enjoy the times talking with me now.

On another occasion, I was talking with the same eight-year-old daughter, listening to her tell me about a birthday party she had been to, when her sister who is ten interrupted to share something since she had been to the same party. When I finished talking with my eight-year-old, she was upset because, as she put it, her sister "stole some of her five minutes" and she wanted "all of her five minutes," so she deserved some more time with me.

Now my wife is even asking me, "What about my five minutes?"

This is great. By taking time to listen, I'm learning about what my children are doing, what they fear and struggle with, and what is important to them.

I recently had a situation where two of my kids were really mad at each other and fighting over some very trivial stuff (in my opinion). I remembered to listen and found out they both had deep hurt and resentment toward each other because of something that they did to each other many years ago. Instead of yelling at them and punishing them for fighting, as I would have done previously, because I took time to listen and understand, I was able to walk them through forgiving each other. It was amazing.

Now my kids are bugging me about "The Celebration" because we have completed the five minutes for five days. They are really enjoying this and I am too.

Thanks, Keith, for sharing your heart with us. Keep spreading the good news to others.

Travis:

I have two boys, very energetic boys like their father, ages four and almost two. My oldest, Rylan, is so compassionate and thoughtful while also commanding a lot of hands-on attention. While we normally get a good amount of time together, what I noticed after your seminar was that "together" was normally with his little brother, Sidney, and/or mom.

Once we started the five minutes for five days, then graduated to the ten minutes for ten days alone, one-on-one (and we're still going strong), I realized quickly that while we had time "together" leading up to this "challenge," it was NOT focused time for Rylan to express himself however he wanted or in whatever activity he wanted.

This realization has really opened up my eyes to see my oldest son as being very particular in what he wants to do. I'm learning that he likes a lot of different things. Some days it's motorcycles, Hot Wheels, and Monster Trucks; the next day it's puzzles, basketball, and the matching game. He is wonderful and really enjoys the I-have-dad-all-to-myself time. He always wants his time alone to be first; we are working on that one.

My younger boy, Sidney, is a little too young to verbalize his feelings and wants but very much understands when I ask him what he wants to do. Some nights it's books: Smash Crash!; Brown Bear, Brown Bear; Tubby Time; etc. At twenty-two months, he is a voracious reader of (or looker at) books and that is all we do some nights. It is alone, quiet time and he eats it up! Then there are his silly play nights where he wants to ride me like a horse, bonk me over the head, and make me fall, then pick me up to do it all over again! He laughs and laughs at this. "Again, again, again," he says.

What I have noticed the most in Sidney is that he is wanting, needing, and seeking Daddy more than he ever has and I love it because I have struggled with bonding with him—way more than with my oldest, Rylan. His new desire to bond has shown itself in the past couple of nights when he has not wanted to be put to bed by my wife (though she is amazing with our boys—absolutely amazing!) and has calmed down for me and snuggled in to read more (and he is NOT a snuggle type!). And then he has rolled over onto my chest to fall asleep! This has never happened since he was born. I LOVE IT!

I finally feel the bonding with Sidney that I had with Rylan at a very early age. This almost brings me to tears writing about it; I have truly been longing for this kind of bond with Sidney and have been frustrated at times that it just hasn't been there. Now, because of the challenge to spend one-on-one time with each of my boys, it's happening.

So thank you for your seminar and sharing your heart with all the men who were there.

Phil:

It has been a tremendous experience to affirm my kids. I have even found myself affirming my wife. On one occasion, I affirmed my mom and sister too. I'm amazed how much this simple technique has helped my confidence to be a better dad. I'm also amazed how God is giving me the words and bringing up memories to affirm my kids.

I have had to work hard at speaking affirmations to my children because it is unnatural for me to do so. I have been trained instead to base conversations and connection with my kids primarily on their performance such as "you did a great job at . . ." or "keep up the good work" rather than "I just love to see you smile and hear your laughter . . ." or "I just love you for being you." This has been a huge eye opener for me. I did not realize how much I was doing this.

Now I am seeing so much more beauty and wonder in each of my kids. I'm trying to stop the performance trap that I have been caught in for so long.

When I can, I have been kissing my sixteen-year-old son on the forehead good night. It was awkward at first, but I wanted to let him know in this way that I love him. I was afraid that he would reject me but he smiles and I know that he is receiving my father love. It's awesome.

I can tell my eleven-year-old daughter I love her. I have grown closer because I am affirming her with written notes and talking with her at bedtime.

I'm still waiting to see changes in and develop a better connection with my thirteen-year-old son. He is the hardest one to reach right now but I will not give up. He is such an awesome kid!

One last thing, I have been blessed by affirming others. This has been a wonderful surprise. I think that God was waiting for me to get to this point. Thank you, Keith, for helping me get here. I am experiencing God's love—his affection and affirmation—in a powerful way. I didn't know how much I needed it.

Conclusion

I wish I could guarantee that if we do all we can as dads, our kids will turn out just as we hope they will. The fact is they are human beings with their own will, separate from ours. We can influence and shape them, but we cannot control them. And it's a really bad idea to try. They will make their own choices. And there will be surprises. Some of those surprises may disappoint us; some will thrill us.

The best we can do is provide them with the security and sense of belonging that deeply loving them and spending lots of time with them should create. In so doing, we hope we've equipped them to handle all that may confront them in life. But we never know. And there are no guarantees. These three endure: love, hope, and faith. But our children's choices will always remain their own. No matter what my boys choose, and whether we are together or apart, I'm committed to loving them, staying actively engaged with them, and supporting them.

Dr. Kyle Pruett nailed it when he wrote, "[Fatherhood] is the single most creative, complicated, fulfilling, frustrating, engrossing, enriching, depleting endeavor of a man's adult life. So often, as [one] reflects on life's rewards, we hear that 'in the final analysis' of money, power, prestige, and marriage, fathering alone was what 'mattered.'"[87]

Throughout my fathering journey, I've many times asked myself questions like the following. Forcing myself to answer them has helped shape me into the father I am today. Some of these sound all-or-nothing, black or white. I don't read them that way. In many cases, the answer can be "both-and." Yet asking these questions as Jerrold Shapiro wrote them forces me to honestly face my own values and discern my heart.[88] I provide them for your benefit as we journey together:

- What kind of dad do I really want to be?
- How do I want my kids to remember me as a dad when they were young?
- Where will I make my greatest impact: at work or with my children?
- Where will I ultimately be most fulfilled?
- If I neglect one for the other, which will I regret the most when I am older?
- Where does it matter to me most that I am successful?
- When all is said and done, how will I define success as a man and as a father?

We've covered a lot of ground together. I've shared the three most influential fathering practices in my life and my healing journey—a skill set and mindset that have shaped me as a father and positively affected my kids. I hope my stories and those of others inspire and empower you in your own journey toward being the dad you long to be.

Here are the main points of the entire book. If you can remember and practice these, you're well on your way to becoming the effective and fulfilled dad you want to be.

- **Love** your children through affirmation, acceptance, and affection.

▸ **Heal** your own father wound.

▸ **Stay focused** on regular, great dad input and taking action.

You Still Matter to Your Children

"No one counts himself great if his children have failed."

— Seneca[89]

When I read Seneca's words, I get a knot in my stomach. I feel the responsibility I have as a dad and my inadequacy for the task. It's a big job to be a great dad. Many men fail, with devastating consequences to their children, to themselves, and to society. They fail not because they try and fall short; they fail by quitting before the job is done, or sometimes before it's even started.

I cling to an ancient Jewish proverb as I stumble along in my fathering: "Love covers all transgressions."[90] I've needed that to be true; I've leaned on it for encouragement when I've blown it with my kids. When I've used harsh words, acted in anger, or hurt my sons' feelings—when I've failed to be the dad I want to be—I remember how much love matters and how much it covers. Kids are resilient and forgiving when they feel loved, even when we haven't acted in a loving way.

Periodic setbacks are essential to personal growth. We cannot fail at being great dads—even when we stumble—unless we give up trying. Mistakes do not make us failures. Part of learning to do it better means making mistakes. Never giving up matters most—being there, again and again and again. Showing up consistently and loving our kids make all the difference. We can do that, even if we don't live with them full time.

I like how psychiatrist and family therapist Frank Pittman says it: "The guys who fear becoming fathers don't understand that fathering is not something perfect men do, but something that perfects the man.

The end product of child raising is not the child but the parent."[91] We are transformed as we engage the fathering journey. Being a dad is not just good for our kids but for us too.

Don't give up, Dad, no matter what has happened so far . . . no matter where you are, whether you live with your kids at this time—or not—whether you're still married to their mom—or not—or ever were.

You still matter to your children. You always will.

A Final Reminder

I leave you with this reminder: becoming a great dad who enjoys remarkably great relationships with your children is one of the most enjoyable and satisfying experiences in life. It's my honor and life's work to help dads achieve that vision—partially through this book and in an ongoing way through The Great Dads Project: our website, other books, CDs, DVDs, training seminars, peak experiences, and coaching. I hope this is the beginning of a long and mutually beneficial relationship. Go to my website now (www.thegreatdadsproject. org), if you've not already done so, and register to be a part of The Community of Dads.

Peace to you.

Be sure to read the epilogue for some additional inspirational father stories.

Remember: Great Dads Shape Great Kids.

Be a great dad today!

Epilogue
It's Worth It!

IN HER BOOK *Father Courage: What Happens When Men Put Family First,* Suzanne Braun Levine writes about what the dads she interviewed want for their children, but she also says that—like you and me—they want something for themselves:

> Educator and writer Allan Shedlin Jr. calls it the experience of "exuberant daddying." He emphasizes the rewards that come with the job.

> Indeed, despite the stress and anxiety and conflict they experienced, the men I interviewed all reported having fun, more fun than they had ever imagined, fun that became joy at unexpected moments. That, in the end, made their choice the only one for them. I see men in loving engagement with their children everywhere—in the hardware store, at the beach, on the bus—and I am sure that even if they aren't doing all they could, they

are different from their fathers. They are also part of something momentous.[92]

That's an important message I want to convey: you are not alone in your desire to become a great dad; millions of other men share your longing. A second message is about how fun this really can be. It's worth it!

There is a growing movement taking shape in our generation: many men are identifying and seeking healing for their father wound and are finding profound fulfillment in their role and identity as fathers. It's not an easy shift, but it's a remarkable one that ultimately produces a deep and long lasting joy.

Near the end of her book, Braun Levine quotes one father of two young sons who says, "I can't believe the incredible amount of work this is. I can't believe the uncategorized, immeasurable, incredible pleasure that it's giving me. They are just tremendous, clear pools of nectar for me and I can't get enough."[93] It really is worth it. More dads are beginning to believe that's true and experience that delight.

In a 1993 book on fathering—in which the culturally relevant examples are a bit outdated but the fathering principles and descriptions are timeless—psychologist Jerrold Lee Shapiro describes a good father in a compelling and perhaps comprehensive way that emphasizes the core elements of a father's affirmation, acceptance, and affection as I've described them: "The good father is available for his children. He is able to show them his interest, love, and caring. He teaches them values by words and by actions. He understands their needs from a child's perspective, yet he maintains his protective parental role. The good father encourages his children to experiment within proper limits. He allows his children to know him well enough that they may incorporate him into their personal psychological selves. He shares with them his pride at their accomplishments and his own. He is always available in times of crisis."

Shapiro then poses this piercing question, "How many men give these gifts to their children?"[94] The answer today, twenty years after his book was published, thankfully, is *millions*. And I'm grateful to say I know some of them personally.

Real-life, personal stories of men who are becoming great dads inspire me. They provide the elevation my own spirit often needs to remind me this fathering journey, identity, and commitment are worth it. Their stories motivate me to keep going.

In this epilogue, I share the stories—in their own words—of some of my friends. I asked each of them to write about their fathering experience—how much they love being a dad and what they feel and think when they reflect on their fathering. I think you're going to enjoy these friends of mine as much as I do. They're just regular, everyday men who are fathers, just like you and me. I hope you'll be as motivated by them and their experiences as I am.

Some of my friends are married; some are not. Some have adopted children; others have biological and stepchildren. Some have sons; others have daughters. Some have babies; others have children who are older; some of their kids are full grown and out of the nest. Some live with their kids; some do not. A few had great dads themselves; many did not. All of them love their kids and are learning to share their affirmation, acceptance, and affection. These are some of the good men in my fathering community who motivate me to be the best dad I can be.

Bobby Colombo

My name is Bobby Colombo, and I love being a father to my two children, Autumn Rose (eleven) and Alex (eight). They are my pride and joy, and my soul delights just thinking of them. I am so glad that I get to be their dad. They help bring healing into my life, as I never had a father. I get to be the dad that I always dreamed of having myself.

Unfortunately, I've made some foolish choices, served a six-year term in prison, but just this past week was granted the blessing of sweet freedom. Although I was heartbroken and utterly devastated over not being able to be the dad I needed to be and for causing pain in my children's precious lives, my prison sentence ended up being the best thing that ever happened to me. I was able to become a much better father from behind prison walls. I learned how I was affected by not having a father and how to ensure that I do not afflict the same deep wound upon my children.

My daughter Autumn is so great. She is very smart and witty and likes to be in school plays. When I talked to her for the first time after my release, she told me that for the past four years she had won first place in a reading contest at her school. I was so proud of her! It made me feel really good to hear that because when I was incarcerated, I used to write her once a week, encouraging her to read, methodically planting seeds.

Autumn's winning the reading contests is a fruit of those seeds. I learned to tell her I was proud of her in my letters. Apparently she listened to my words, and they had a profound impact on her because after she told me how she won the reading contests, I said to her, "I am so proud of you sweetie." She said, "I know, Dad."

When she said that, my eyes filled with tears of joy. I love to talk to her for hours now that I'm free to do so. And, perhaps more importantly, I love to listen to her too.

My boy Alex is like a "mini-me." I love him so much, and I believe in him. I know that he needs me to be his dad. He makes me laugh, and I love spending time with him. I am going to teach him how to ride a skateboard, and he wants me to show him how to play football.

My children mean the world to me. They are the true treasures of life. After having my freedom taken away, I was able to see all the things I took for granted. In prison, I learned to appreciate things more, especially my children. I am so glad that prison is behind me now and that I can move forward and use the new tools I have learned that will help me be a great dad.

I am a living testimony that shows no matter how bad you have messed up, it is never too late to start being a dad. I did not see my children the entire time I was in prison but I can tell you my words through weekly letters had a great impact on them. Yours can too. Your kids need you! If you are reading this book, and you've made it this far, then you are already a good dad for taking the time to do so.

Bill Meyer

I wanted to be a dad almost as long as I can remember. For years, I thought and prayed about how wonderful it would be—all through my teens, my twenties, my thirties, and into my forties. I was often told that I'd make a great dad, but almost all of my friends became dads before I did. Finally, at age forty-four, I got married to the woman of my dreams. We adopted our son, Evan, when I was forty-five. Ellie was born when I was forty-six. Now, three years later, I look back and realize how little I knew about the challenges and the joys of fatherhood.

In my early adult years, while my peers enjoyed "hitting the town," "spreading their wings," and "playing the field," my comfort zone was in spending time with family and close friends. There were no nieces or nephews until recently, but there were always friends' kids around, and I was often referred to as their "Uncle Bill."

My proudest young adult moments were becoming a godfather on two occasions, being invited to experience a good friend's son being born, and a ten-plus year relationship as a Big Brother to a wonderful boy—now a wonderful man! While I loved family and wanted my own, I also formed parental theories that were naïve and simplistic and developed a judging attitude toward parents who weren't doing it right (so I thought). I also carried a great deal of bitterness from my own broken relationship with my father.

I grew up in a middle-class suburban home, a home that had an abundance of love and acceptance—from my mother. My mom was one of the most loving, selfless people I've ever met. She had an advanced college degree, but she left her career at a young age to raise me, my two brothers, and my sister. I now know how hard she worked to raise four kids, but she never let it show. While we fought, bickered, and pushed many boundaries, my mom gave a seemingly endless amount of love, patience, and support.

Though Mom gave so much, there was no loving marriage being modeled, and my dad was emotionally and often physically absent. Both my parents drank heavily when I was very young. My mom was able to quit while my dad wasn't. I'm thankful Dad wasn't an angry, violent drunk; he was more of a checked-out drunk.

For reasons that were hard to understand then, but make sense now, my dad's distance caused huge problems in my parents' marriage and in our family. I have almost no memories of my parents getting along. As my dad drank more, the marriage further deteriorated. My dad started spending every Saturday on the golf course, then came prolonged business trips, then extramarital affairs. When I was in college, my parents divorced.

The absence of my father for much of my upbringing had a huge impact on my transition into manhood. I never received my father's approval or blessing. I believe he loved me, but he never communicated it with words or actions. There was not a single "I love you" and there were very few words of encouragement, pride, or acceptance.

Because he was gone so much, there was little teaching, modeling, or helping, and I was left to experience the transition to manhood on my own. I carried what were normal teenage insecurities well into adulthood. As those insecurities faded, I began to resent my father for his absences and his unfaithfulness to my mom and our family. I was angry, and I wanted to prove to myself that I could be a better parent than my dad had been.

Many years passed, and I experienced many failed relationships. Finally, I met and married Molly. We both wanted children, but we were older newlyweds than most, and we each had a heart for adoption. Six months after we were married, in what we can only explain as a gift from a gracious God, we were connected through friends to a woman who lived 2,000 miles away. She was three months pregnant and wanted to put her child up for adoption.

We expressed interest, and after a few months of waiting without word, we met and enjoyed getting to know Alison, the birth mom. She invited us to several doctor appointments and then to Evan's birth. He was born a beautiful, healthy, redheaded boy. Two days later, we brought him home from the hospital. Our relatively simple but very emotional adoption process was over, and our lives as proud, blessed parents began.

The first few months as older new parents felt as if our world was turned upside down. We had no idea how many things we had taken for granted, such as sleep, quiet, and flexibility. Midway through Evan's first year, things started to settle down and we began gaining some confidence in our new roles. Today at nearly four years old, Evan is so energetic and full of life. He's a squirmer more than a sitter, a runner more than a walker, and a climber more than a talker. He's sensitive, and he has an engaging smile that will light up any room. Although we didn't give him his genetic code, we have a special love for him that is unconditional and unending.

Six months after Evan's birth and adoption, we got the surprise of our lives—Molly was pregnant! After a fairly easy pregnancy and a very difficult birth, we had our beautiful and wonderful daughter Elise, whom we call Ellie. Ellie looks a bit like her mom, even a bit like her brother, but people say she looks a lot like her dad. Ellie is now two and a half and has a very different personality from her brother's. She is much more of a sitter and a talker. She has a charming and loving presence, and it melts this daddy's heart when she burrows her head into my neck and shoulder and says "Daddy, Daddy, Daddy."

Being a father has brought me love, companionship, stability, and a heightened sense of meaning and purpose. Equally important, it's helped me to better understand myself and to grow more than I ever imagined. I've surrendered many of my overly simplistic ideals and now realize that parenting well is difficult. Surely, boundaries and grace are both important, but so is consistency.

Being present to support my wife and teach my kids cannot be compromised, but neither can my role as financial provider. Although there are no easy answers, I long to father based on principles, specifically practicing faith, being together, and having fun. It's a joy to see some practices work, and I'm fortunate to have Molly point out the ones that don't.

I thank God regularly for the opportunity to be the father of two wonderful kids. They are growing every day, and I know I am too. I feel I have so much to appreciate, so much to give, and so much to learn—but thankfully no longer anything to prove. I've been able to let that go now. I love my life as a father.

Graham Scharf

I'm wired to be an achiever. Give me a problem, and I'll solve it; give me a goal, and I'll exceed it. I never dreamed of being a father because I didn't think it was important. It was a part of life, to be sure, but a peripheral part of being an achiever.

It was a very good thing that I had the privilege of fathering thrust upon me because I would have chosen achievement over children. My wife, Rebecca, gave birth to our firstborn daughter, Elisabeth, when we were only twenty-five and still in the midst of higher education. She was in her fourth year of medical school, and I was teaching full-time in a failing elementary school while completing my final year of a Master of Arts in Teaching.

Our life situation gave us three options. We could pay someone else to provide childcare; Rebecca could be the full-time parent; or I could be the full-time parent. With a grueling residency that could demand as many as one hundred hours a week still ahead of Rebecca, we realized that if we both worked, we would have little or no family time for the next three years.

Alternately, if she stayed home with Elisabeth, it would be far more difficult to do a residency later in life. Without a residency, she wouldn't be able to practice medicine at all. By contrast, I had experience in a successful consulting team and an advanced degree in education. I could step out of the workforce and step back in with relative ease. Becoming a full-time father was, from our perspective, the only viable option.

We lived in New York City at the time, the mecca of achievers. One of the first questions in a conversation with a new acquaintance at a playground or at a cocktail party is almost inevitably, "So, what do you do?" Among my peers, the answers range from investment banking to medicine to running a start-up or nonprofit. Everyone does something remarkable. And then the question comes to me, "So, what do you do?"

I remember well that when I first became a full-time father, I told people what I *had* done in consulting and education and then concluded, "And now I'm home with my daughter." Fatherhood, as much as I enjoyed it, still didn't measure up on the achiever index.

When Elisabeth was about four years old, I discovered *Honey for a Child's Heart: The Imaginative Use of Books in Family Life*. In those pages, Gladys Hunt introduced me to the rich world of enjoying children's literature *with* children. We went to the library and checked out stacks of books from the book list (which comprises the entire second half of the book) and sat together on the floor with *Curious George*, *Olivia the Pig*, and *Lilly's Big Day and her Purple Plastic Purse*, among others.

I called my parents and announced, "I have found the best book on children's literature!" They replied, "Did you know that we used that book to find books for you when you were little?" Their investment in me was now coming full circle as I began to relish fatherhood even more in the context of great books, combining my love for books and education with my love for fathering my daughter. When Elisabeth turned five, I read her the *Chronicles of Narnia* and the *Little House on the Prairie* series, and we both loved every minute.

I have been a full-time father for five years, and we now have a second beautiful daughter, Katherine. I have come to both see and feel that being a father is not peripheral to achievement. A successful author and friend put it this way: "My books are popular now. In twenty years, I don't know whether anyone will remember my books. But I do know that I'll have a relationship with my kids."

Relationships matter. My relationships with my daughters matter a lot more than my current employment, which I can almost certainly predict will not be my job in twenty years. Now when I'm asked, "So, what do you do?" I usually simply reply, "I'm a father." My achievement index has been adjusted. It isn't just that I have the privilege of being a *full-time* father; it is that I have the privilege of being a father.

Tom Tsao

Back in the 1960s, my parents immigrated from Taiwan to the United States with only $500 and a couple of suitcases to their names to pursue the American Dream. I was born in New York—their only child. Growing up in an immigrant family wasn't easy. Acclimating to a new culture and language without a financial safety net made for stressful times during my childhood. With the best intentions, my dad put intense pressure on me to do well in school so I could go to a top Ivy League college and eventually get a stellar job and make a lot of money. After all, this was the whole point of pursuing the American Dream.

This intense focus on achievement orientation, however, had its drawbacks for my relationship with my dad. It felt as if his love for me was conditional on my accomplishments—that my dad would love me only if I did well. Unfortunately, even though I ended up doing well, I never grew close to my dad; there isn't a level of affection or intimacy between us. While I understand the financial and cultural pressures he faced as a first-generation immigrant that might have motivated him to raise me that way, I do feel a significant loss of intimacy in my relationship with my dad.

My father is an atheist, and despite how he raised me, I decided to believe in and follow God as a young adult. I experienced unconditional love from God. I believe God loves me regardless of what I have done (good or bad). I learned that my identity as God's son was completely independent of my behaviors or accomplishments. What a paradigm shift: identity does not equal behavior.

This shift has changed my attitude about life and has given me an entirely new perspective on raising my own two daughters (now ages eight and five). While I can at times be disappointed in their behavior, I always have joy in their identities as my daughters regardless of what they do or don't do. This doesn't mean that I don't expect them to do their best, but it means that I want them to know that I will always love them regardless of how they perform.

I also feel that instead of pressuring them to do something I think they "should" do, I am committed to be in a journey of discovering with them how God has created each of them and to help them "incline" in that direction rather than forcing them to do something they weren't created to do.

While I enjoy spending time with my wife and daughters as a family together, I especially cherish the special one-on-one dates that I have with each of my daughters. Even though they are only eight and five, I want them each to have individual, focused attention and time with me so they know the love of their dad and get special daddy time. This tradition is something I look forward to continuing with my daughters well into their adulthood. I intend for our dates to get a bit fancier as they get older because I want them to experience what a fancy date with a real gentleman is like. This way when the time comes for a young man who intends to take one of my daughters out on a romantic date, she won't be easily impressed, bedazzled, or swept off her feet by the first knight in shining armor that comes along.

She will also know how a real gentleman should treat her on a date, so she will know exactly how she should be treated and won't accept any compromising situations. I'm praying for all you dads with sons out there that you will do similarly when you spend time with your sons—that you will teach them how to be real gentlemen.

I am also wholly committed to telling my daughters how much I love them and showing my affection to them as their daddy. It's critically important that I don't bottle up my love for them and keep it to myself, but instead I am committed to clearly expressing the overflowing of joy, love, playfulness, and intimacy that I feel for them. I want them to feel cherished and secure in the closeness of our relationships.

I also believe that if my daughters don't get the affirmation, love, and affection from their dad that they need, they will end up feeling some emptiness and may look for those things in the arms of other men in less appropriate ways.

I thank God for my daughters and the opportunity to be a father to them. The unconditional love I experience from God is the kind of unconditional love I am hoping to pass on to them. It has also been an interesting experience to have my own dad see how I raise my daughters. I see a softer side of him when he is with them that I never experienced myself when I was a child. I often see him unabashedly exclaiming, "Abby, I looooove you!" Who is this man? My mom and I don't recognize him. It's sweet.

I'm grateful and now believe that trying to be a great dad is certainly a far more rewarding experience than a soulless, loveless pursuit of the American Dream.

Mike Bauer

I'll be turning fifty this year, but my children are only four and seven. I was a late bloomer as far as becoming a dad. To be honest, through the earlier years of my adulthood, I never felt a huge need or desire to get married and become a dad. Looking back, I think this was a subconscious response to my own experience of growing up in a very dysfunctional environment. Even though my parents stayed married for twenty-five years before divorcing, their relationship was never good, even from the start.

To keep things concise, let's just say that my father has never told me he loves me. I don't think he ever hugged me until I was twenty-two years old, when I had just received my black belt in karate after several grueling hours of testing.

To be fair, I did feel valued because I always got the best of everything. My dad was a successful contractor. We were on the affluent side of things, and I was always given the resources to pursue whatever endeavor I was interested in. It just seemed my parents were unable to outwardly show their hearts to me or to my siblings. This was especially true of my dad.

The bittersweet thing in all this is that my dad gave me the opportunity to work in a successful family business. Even though my interests lay elsewhere, the pull toward the relatively easier road to a monetarily successful life was too great. So I started a life in construction at an early age. I worked on my dad's job sites during summer vacations from school. This continued through college until I started full-time in the office at the age of twenty-four. Over the years I learned more and more about running the company. I have never had a job outside the family business.

When my dad retired in 1999, I took over the company with my brother, and we ran it very successfully until about 2008, when the recession hit us hard. The reason for this back-story is to illustrate how much our family business had become my identity. Basically "I" was a successful company. It was all I ever knew, even though running the family business was never really a passion for me.

I met Linh in 2000, and we were married two years later. Fast forward a few years and we had two cute kids running around the house. Because of the demands of my company, I typically left the house for my office at 5:45 AM and would get home around 5:30 PM or so. I never had a chance to see the kids in the morning, which disappointed me. When I would get home, I was typically so exhausted that it was difficult to engage with my family for quite a while. During this time, Linh and I had an ongoing prayer that I would be open to a new direction.

Around March of 2009, the recession was in full swing in California, and company sales had diminished to about 30 percent of normal. I needed to make a next step decision regarding my business. Option one was to double my efforts and time within the company to try to maintain my income level, which would leave even less time for my family than I already had. Option two was to do something quite contrary to my self-sufficient instincts, and that was to trust that we were receiving the answer to our prayers: I was to invest my energy in a new direction.

We made the tough decision that instead of working even harder in the company to get sales back up, I would actually scale back and invest myself for this season with my kids. We would live mostly on my wife's income. She is a successful dentist with her own practice and is able to work just four days a week.

We decided to keep my company open, but I would focus only on working with existing accounts and not spend an inordinate amount of time chasing new projects. This would leave me with much more time to focus on my family.

I can't explain how hard it was to let go of something to which my identity and ego were so tied. Now it's equally difficult to explain the joy of spending so much quantity and quality time involved with and watching my children blossom. Their own self-image and confidence as they develop and grow are a joy to behold. I believe to a large extent their self-image and confidence are strong because they have two parents who are present to them. Mom has always been there, and now so is Dad to a greater degree than ever. I'm not an expert in child development by any means, but I believe there is a special need that a child has for his or her "Daddy." I am so grateful that I'm able to provide it.

I was recently with my daughter at a classmate's birthday party. As I was talking with one of the other dads, he said, "Rachel is the happiest kid in her class. Everyone always wants to play with her because she is always in such a good mood." Hearing words like that fill my heart, and they are worth so much more than any amount of money I could have made working extra long hours trying to raise my income to prerecession levels.

As Linh and I prepared to have kids, we shared a hope that "the dysfunction would end here." I've had to work through issues due to a lack of good parenting. I know my parents had similar or even worse experiences. I imagine there have been generations of wounding. Linh and I hope that starting with our children there will be generations of healthy, well-adjusted kids who grow to reach their full potential as human beings in the future.

I know I'm not a perfect dad in any way, but now I feel our hope is closer to the truth than ever. As I said, our kids are blossoming. So is my joy as their dad.

Jerry Hall

When I was nineteen years old, my parents gathered together my two older brothers, my younger sister, and me and told us they were separating and that my mom and sister were moving away. My parents explained to us they never loved each other; the only reason they stayed together for twenty-two years was for us.

I was stunned. I then felt angry and later guilty. I somehow felt responsible for my parents' unhappy "sacrifice." I made a vow: I would never stay in a miserable marriage just for the sake of my kids. Eight years and three sons later, I fulfilled my vow. I left my marriage and young boys.

I am now eighteen years into my fourth (and final) marriage. It has taken years of counseling and personal growth for me to understand the way I have lived my life, the choices I've made, and the relationships I have damaged. I came to forgive my parents and chose to seek the forgiveness of those I hurt. Though some consequences endure, I'm now so grateful for the opportunity to be the husband and dad I wish I could have always been.

One of the ways I avoided dealing with the pain I had caused my first wife and my three sons (and myself) was to throw myself into what became a successful career. I climbed the corporate ladder to vice president of marketing. With the support of my current wife, I then literally put everything on the line. With only three months of savings, we moved in with her parents to start my own technology company.

In the midst of the long process of getting funding for my company, my wife shared the news she was pregnant. It took a while for this news to sink in. My first thought was, "We'd better get this company funded!"

By the time my daughter was born, my company had raised millions of dollars in venture capital and already had forty employees. We were well into building our product. While many people I know (including myself at the time) would liken starting a new company to "giving birth," the day my daughter was born made that a ridiculous comparison for me. In a significant way, I was (re)born that day as well. I now had a second chance to become the dad I had never been.

For many years, I had lived a bifurcated life: successful in my professional career, a failure in my personal life. I blew my first opportunity to be a dad. Like many other men who have failed in this way, I did not believe I deserved another chance. But on February 9, 1998, my daughter was born, and suddenly everything changed for me. I no longer cared as much about having a successful career or company. I wanted to be a good father.

After my daughter was born, I would look down at her sleeping early in the morning before heading off to yet another twelve- to fifteen-hour day at work, and tears would form in my eyes. My initial dream of building a company had been replaced with the reality of being the dad of a "Precious Princess." After four months of this misery, without clearly knowing (or caring) how much money I'd be giving up, I left the company I started in my in-laws' laundry room to pursue my new passion.

I made a new vow: I will never leave my daughter (and soon thereafter, my fourth son) no matter how "bad" my marriage was. I'm thankful that after years of learning and effort, I now have the best marriage and family I could imagine. I realize now how thoughtless and selfish my first vow was. I have faced a number of deep issues that I had either not known about or had been avoiding.

I am now the father of four sons, (James, Gabriel, Michael, and Kieran) and a daughter (Camryn). My three older boys are grown; my fourth son and only daughter are growing. They have a mom and dad who love them more than anything. My two oldest sons by far experienced the most pain from my abandoning my first family. While I have sought and received forgiveness and much healing, some of that pain continues to this day.

Nearly three years ago, the youngest of my first three sons was to be married to his high school sweetheart. As most dads would be, I felt proud and happy for him. About two weeks before the wedding, a difficult realization hit me—this should be a proud moment for a dad after years of raising his son and preparing him for adulthood. My son getting married should have been my official launching of him into the start of his own family. But it occurred to me that I didn't raise him—he was actually raised by his mom and stepdad. I had almost no participation. It was a very painful reminder of another lingering consequence.

I decided to call his mom and tell her what I was feeling. After listening sympathetically she said, "I was wondering when this would hit you." I decided to write a letter to my son's stepdad to thank him for the great job he did raising my son. The wedding turned out to be a wonderful event. I believe additional healing took place at that time for me and for Michael, my third son.

My two oldest sons, who did have me as a dad for their early years, are both now in their thirties; neither is married. I'm not sure why, but I think the example I set for them early on has hurt and frightened them.

My wife and I are now approaching our eighteenth wedding anniversary; our daughter Camryn is thirteen, and our son Kieran is eleven.

Last year, Camryn started playing in junior golf tournaments. For her first five events, I walked the course with her and encouraged her while she played. Before the tournament, we reviewed each hole and made notes on her scorecard about which club she would hit off the tee, where the hazards were, etc.

Then a tournament came up that I wasn't able to attend. It was on a course that she hadn't played before. I called her afterward to find out how she did. She came in third place. I asked her what her process was for figuring out which club to hit. Her reply floored me. She said, "Every time it was my turn to hit the ball, I would think to myself, what would my dad do?"

My new vow has resulted in a truly fulfilled life: I now have a great marriage, and I get to raise two kids I adore and with whom I am actively engaged. I'll leave it up to my kids to decide whether I'm a "great dad," but what I know is that I am definitely a "lucky dad."

Chris Helwig

I have two wonderful daughters I adore: Lauren, age nine, and Abby, who is seven. They're growing up way too fast.

You never know when a special moment will occur, sometimes when you least expect it. I took Lauren out to dinner the other evening with one of my friends, Jerry Hall, and his daughter, as well as some of Lauren's friends. Since I hadn't seen Jerry in a while, the meal lasted quite some time. Sitting at the dinner table, and even eating in general, is not Lauren's favorite thing to do. She is athletic (which is very fun for me) and likes to keep moving and doing lots of things. Eating is not one of them.

When we were driving home after the dinner, just the two of us, Lauren spoke up from the back seat and spontaneously said, "I love you, Daddy." I wasn't expecting that from her, yet I could tell it came from her heart. I did not prompt it, nor did our conversation. Though it happened in a moment, I know it is one of those cherished memories that will last a lifetime for me. I choose to embrace the words and the wonderful feeling it gave me. I will always have it as a gift.

I felt such a deep joy and gratitude for being Lauren's dad that evening. What could be better than hearing your daughter tell you she loves you, not because she wanted to get anything, because she was supposed to, or because she had to, but just because it was real to her in that moment, and she wanted to express her heart. I love that.

I thought to myself, this is what it's all about. By choosing to invest my time, love, and energy in my daughter, correcting her, encouraging her, and above all else, letting her know that I will always be here for her and that I love her, I have built a deep and enduring relationship with her. She knows that I love her not for what she does, not because she is a good athlete and has already accomplished much in sports and in school; I love her for who she is, my precious daughter—my one and only Lauren, a gift God has given me to love and raise.

Abby is my younger daughter. She has a very easygoing "it's all good" type of attitude. She is always humming to herself when she plays, and she does very well just playing by herself with her imagination and her pet shop or zoom-zoom pets.

Abby is our cuddler, and I love to hug her. She and I have developed a playful game where she now runs away from my hugs, and I have to chase her to catch her and hug her. I can tell when Abby gets in her "Daddy mode," and the game is about to begin, or she just needs "Daddy time." Then I'll hear her say, "Daddy, look at this," "Daddy, can you play this with me," "Daddy, come look what I did."

It's wonderful. I know this is her way of connecting, and I love it. Since it's on her time schedule and I don't know when it's going to happen, I try to savor each moment. I attempt to set aside anything I am doing, if I can (and I usually can), to spend those moments with her, to be the daddy she needs and longs for, to show her by my attentiveness that her interests are important to me, and to demonstrate that her daddy adores and fully enjoys being with her.

Abby is always fully engaged in whatever she does, and in those special moments when she invites me into her world, I get to be a part of that full engagement. What could be better and more enjoyable than that? I get to share in her world for a moment.

I want to savor these special relational moments forever. It fills me up with joy. I get to let the rest of the world slip away for a short time, and it's just Abby and me. It's a magical place because I am now a part of her imaginary world that she loves. She is creating a place in her mind, and she wants me in it. It's a place I want to be. When I'm there, I get to see how she sees things and how the world works for her. It's a gift to get a glimpse of my daughter's world and mind. The innocence and sense of magic is something that uplifts my heart and bonds me to my daughter in a special way, in a special place, forever.

Steve Dershimer

My wife Elizabeth and I had been married for a dozen years when we decided the time was right to begin the process of uniting with a child to call our own. After many months of planning and waiting, we traveled to Ethiopia in August 2010 to meet our adopted daughter. On a Friday afternoon at a beloved, window-lit care center, Tesfanesh was carefully placed in Elizabeth's arms. We call her Tessa. She was nine months old. Her white, oversized socks scrunched against her new mother's hip.

In those first moments together, she looked at us with unblinking eyes and tight lips. When we held her, she would often crane back her neck to look us in the eyes. She would even straighten her arms to watch us square on. It wasn't until a sweet "nah-nee" (a care provider at the center) handed us a sippy cup of avocado juice to give to her that she smiled and embraced us.

The few days at the hotel in Addis Ababa followed by the twenty-seven-hour plane ride back to the States sealed our initial bond. Tessa experienced diarrhea and two ear infections on that trip. When we walked off the plane in Phoenix, we were down to our very last diaper and her final article of clothing from the diaper bag. Slogged with less than four hours of sleep and wearing smelly, dank clothes of my own, I smiled at my initiation into fatherhood.

Early on at home, I felt as though Tessa had been my daughter for thousands of years. At least it seemed it had been in the making for that long. I am not a religious person, yet I know we were made to span time together. When I held her, she would often grab my left ear, then slide her fingers back and forth on my lobe. It was final and sure: Elizabeth and I are here for her innate need for comfort. We hope to be the source of wholeness and finality in her short life thus far.

For the past year, Tessa and I have spent most days together. We've run hundreds of miles together (well, she in stroller) and spent countless hours in various parent group classes at the library and at My Gym, a child-centered fitness class. The park and ball games also frame sweet time getting to know this life together. Routine, time, and space ground our relationship—building and evolving the natural dynamic I've always wanted in a relationship with a child.

I see this symbolized in a specific activity we share every day—and have since she's been home with us. We retrieve the mail daily. A year ago when we started, I pushed her in the stroller and placed the mail in her lap. Then after a bit, I carried her (and the mail on the return walk back to the house). After a few months of that, she walked part of the trip herself. Then she held the mail key and walked.

Now, she walks all the way and assists in pushing and twisting the key into the slot. Last week we decided to measure the distance between our house and the mailboxes down the street. She held one end of the tape measure half the way then decided she wanted to chalk the markers. It was 132 yards—but probably longer.

We don't share blood or genes, but I couldn't feel closer to a biological daughter. I'm not sure how this happened, but we are now pressed together as our hands are when we tool around our community for fun, errands, and adventure.

When we are in our home or in the car—alone—she is simply my daughter, and that's it. However, when we go out, I am reminded she is *adopted*. I am sympathetic to this. I am a tall, balding Caucasian, and she's an African beauty with lavish and squiggly locks atop her curious head.

It's 11:15 on a Tuesday morning, and we are cruising Target. People want to know what's up. I don't blame them. If I saw us, I would look or smile or squint too! Once, we were playing "hide and seek" at Barnes and Noble, and I noticed an older African American man and his eyes sternly set on us. I eventually said "hello" to him, and Tessa blew him a kiss (which she does copiously to pretty much anyone she notices looking at her). He took his toothpick out of his mouth and said, "You two are sure something to look at." I guess we probably are, but we are set together: I am her dad, and she is my daughter.

I have friends who ask me how I feel about not having a bio-logical child. My answer seems to rile them. I say, "I am relieved it didn't happen." I feel I was made to adopt. I am a self-absorbed type of soul and the thought of having a child genetically linked to me makes my brain ache. I am so much like my father, and I think about that every day. I purge the stuff I don't want and accentuate what I like about him.

For better or for worse, I always work on being a whole and healthy person. I am sensitive and mostly live in my head. Being mindful and in the moment is paramount. Sure, I have expectations and desires for how Tessa develops and grows into a girl and woman—a balanced human being. Without the genetic relation, however, I am free to be undivided in the sense I am unfettered to wonder whether she will be like me psychologically and emotionally, as I am so much like my own father. My worth is not set in her. At least so far, I don't have the sense that her success reflects on me.

Tessa turns two in a few days. I have only been her father for a little more than a year. I have seen her take first steps and utter first words, and I picked her up after her first tumble and wiped her fresh tears. I received the ball from her first kick, throw, and header. I wait for her when she sprawls out on the tile, crying over disappointment. I'm running to her room when she wakes from a nightmare and cries, "HOLD YOU, HOLD YOU."

And as we grow together, I will teach her pronouns and the many other gifts and tools she'll need in the world when she leaves our nest. She'll take away some of that stuff, but I imagine among the most meaningful "take-aways" for her will be her own impressions of who I am as a person—how she experienced me as a man and as a father.

Though I've never purchased a lottery ticket in my life, being Tessa's dad feels as if I won millions. The prize is I get to be her father, and I do so with enthusiasm and gratitude. I cleave to Tessa as my daughter.

Jeff Boswell

Given what I now know as an adult—how few men experienced their own dads as a warm, loving, strong presence throughout their childhood—I feel fortunate to have had such a great dad for so many years of my life. My dad was available to me and to my sister and showed interest in us and love to us. He taught us values by what he said and what he lived. He encouraged us to experiment in life, but he always set protective limits. He helped us know him, which allowed us to take the best of him into our own psychological selves. He was always proud of our accomplishments and shared his own. I loved my dad. And I know he loved me.

Although Dad had a job that involved a lot of travel, he was still actively engaged with me. He told me stories that had moral values that he wanted to teach me, even when I was too young to know what he was doing. He laid a strong foundation for the development of my personality and character. He was involved in everything I did. I grew up playing baseball and basketball. I played a lot of games over the years. My dad never missed one.

One time, he told me he couldn't make one of my all-star games because he was in Florida for a meeting. I told him I understood, though I was disappointed because I was pitching that night. As I was warming up for the game, Dad came walking into the park, yelling to me, "Go get 'em." Dad left his meeting before it was over, caught an earlier flight, and then drove nearly three hours to make sure he was there. As a kid, I couldn't fully appreciate the effort he made, though I was happy to see him. Now that I'm a dad myself, I realize what he did and the sacrifice he made, and I appreciate him even more.

Having grown up with such a great dad left huge shoes to fill when I became a dad. As I grew, he encouraged me to move out into the world to be my own man. I got married and had twin sons. Dad taught me right from wrong in many areas of life. He taught me and showed me how to treat a wife and how to always be there for my kids. Even still, after eight years of marriage, when my boys were only four years of age, I had to do the hardest thing I had ever done in my life: I had to tell my mom and dad I was getting divorced.

My parents were the perfect couple; they did everything together. They would argue every now and then, but I always knew they loved each other, and they always resolved their difficulties. To look them in the eye and tell them I failed was brutal. That conversation will never leave my memory, partially because of how afraid I was and partially because how my fears melted away when my dad responded. He said he knew we were having problems. *How?* I wondered. I had never said a thing; I was too ashamed.

He was firm when he told me that we had two boys and that remaining their parents was essential. He wanted to make sure we tried every avenue to work things out. He paid for counseling. He and Mom took my wife and me to dinner and talked with us. Though we weren't able to save our marriage and family, my dad helped us realize we had to make sure we kept our kids' best interests at heart. My ex-wife and I still talk regularly about the boys so that we are as consistent in our parenting as possible. Our boys see this and appreciate it.

When I became a divorced dad of twin, four-year-old boys, I was scared. I would not be able to kiss my sons every night. I missed them. I cherished the time I did have with them and wanted to make the most of every minute. The main thing I did was to make sure they knew that I loved them and that the divorce wasn't their fault.

I also stayed involved in their lives. I went to their school and ate lunch with them two or three times a week. That allowed me to meet their friends and to talk with their teachers. I coached their baseball teams and basketball teams. When they were old enough, I got them a cell phone. We would talk and text several times a day (and still do). Even though I didn't see them every day, I was involved in their lives.

One mistake I made early on was that when I did have them with me, I'd make it a party. We did fun things, we went to movies, played baseball, and went to eat. I soon realized I was trying to be their friend and forgot that I was their dad. I had to make sure that they knew about discipline, the importance of homework, and rules and expectations. I was surprised that our relationship got better. It's hard to be a divorced dad, but I made it work. It took more effort, but the rewards have been worth it.

Four years after my divorce, I remarried. I married a wonderful woman who had a daughter from her first marriage. We then added our own daughter together. Today we have a blended family of two seventeen-year-old sons, a twelve-year-old daughter, and a seven-year-old daughter. The girls live with us full time; the boys do not. Having a family of mine, hers, and ours and blending them into a family together takes daily effort. It sure isn't easy, but it sure is worth the effort.

We establish rules, and we try to raise all our kids in a loving home. We attempt to be involved in everything they do. As I get older, I catch myself saying things my parents said to me as a child. I also grow to appreciate and respect all they went through and the sacrifices they made for me when I was younger.

I'm not a perfect father. I've made mistakes. And I made decisions that in retrospect I regret, but I always had my kids' best interests at heart. I'm sure my dad didn't make every correct decision, but I never knew. The most important thing is that he left a legacy of fatherhood to me that I am trying to instill in my kids. I want them to be great fathers and mothers. If we can foster that legacy, that's the greatest gift I can give. And it's a way of saying thank you to my great dad.

My dad passed away four years ago on Father's Day. Though he is gone, his legacy as a great dad and grandfather will always be with me and with my children.

Jon Lachelt

I remember following a father and daughter into a hardware store many years ago. They were both tall; she looked to be an older high school age girl, maybe even in college, and she was holding his hand. She was obviously at ease, and that simple attachment suggested a deep trust and fondness between them. I sent up a prayer that my daughter would also be proud to walk with me and hold my hand even when she was grown.

Now it's many years later, and I have three more daughters than I did then. I'm grateful that all of them will take my hand at various times—even in public. I absolutely love those moments that reveal I have a sweet daughter who is proud of her daddy. If I have any doubts about the relationship that we've developed over time and that my girls are comfortable with who they are and with the strength of our bond, they are quickly dispelled in these simple and special moments.

As my daughters were growing up, I drove them to school most days. Early on I got into the habit of getting out with them to open the hatch to get their things and give them a quick shoulder hug and a kiss on the forehead. When I started dropping my eldest off at high school, I wondered whether that would change. Would that embarrass her? It warmed my heart when she told me that she still liked me hugging and kissing her good-bye. She said it didn't embarrass her but made her feel cherished.

I've done lots of things wrong in my parenting, and still do, but my girls know that I love them and cherish them. The words of the Jewish proverb are so true: "Love covers a multitude of transgressions."

How do my girls know that I love them? Well, of course, I tell them, but I also try to show them in as many ways as possible. I give a quick back rub when they seem stressed; I read out loud to them; I help them with their homework; I read some of the books that they like; I go into their bedrooms to tell them good night (even when they say, "You don't need to put me to bed tonight").

I make them eat their vegetables; I help them decide how to spend their money; I make them honey-lemon tea when they have a sore throat; I encourage them to get exercise; I include the things they care about in our mealtime or nighttime prayers; I honor their mother; I check up on their grades in school; I take them shopping for a new dress and tell them what I like and what I think is too revealing; I help maintain our family traditions that they enjoy; and I take them to a yearly father-daughter dance in our town.

I like doing all of these things, but I'll admit there are times when I'd rather not do some of them. Being a good dad is hard work, but when it feels hard, I remind myself to look forward to the reward of seeing my daughters grown-up—confident in their womanhood and in their abilities and aware that their dad is behind them and wants the best for them.

Now my oldest daughter is getting ready to go away (a long way) to college this fall, and I can truly say that I am thrilled for her. I'll miss her a great deal. I wish I could be there to share in the new ways that she'll experience the world. I'm so thankful for the years we've had together and excited to see what kind of a blessing she will be to the rest of the world. At the same time, I wonder what the new family dynamic will be with her gone. I do know that I'm looking forward to being able to spend more time with my three other precious girls and to show them how much I cherish each of them.

Cory Ishida

The Lord blessed me with three wonderful daughters. They are all so special and so different. That is one of the things we fathers need to remember. Each child is special and uniquely made by God, so we must raise them accordingly.

For instance, I would take my daughters out on their birthdays— just "daddy and me time." I took Tiffany, my oldest, on her fifth birthday to Charley Brown's. Her mom dressed her up in a beautiful long dress, and we had an incredible time. When I asked her after dinner how she liked it, she said, "I wish we went to McDonald's." Later, in her teen years, Tiffany then loved to go to places that were beautiful for her dinner. I think it made her feel special.

My second daughter, Sunday, is extremely relational and always has been. Whenever she was around, the family was always engaged. She was the straw that stirred the drink. She was also the Post-it queen. Everywhere she went, there was a Post-it note. Open my dresser drawer and there was a Post-it note from Sunday. Come home from work, and there was a Post-it note somewhere. Whenever I was around Sunday, I needed to stop and listen because she always had something to say. Listening to her intently made her feel special.

My youngest, Bethany, grew up being my buddy. We watched football together. We played ball together. For her birthday dinner, she always loved to go to a steakhouse. We have been to the best steakhouses in southern California together. Bethany and I would strategize together—whether it was in participating in sports, playing games, or figuring out how to get somewhere. Thinking, planning, and executing the plan together made her feel special.

I think that is one of the things that is so important for us dads is to make all our children feel special in their own way. Come to think of it, as I tried to make them feel special, they always returned the favor. Whenever I am in their presence, I feel special—always did, still do.

Phil Mickelson

I want to share one more real-life story from a dad who is not a friend of mine, though I'd sure be happy to meet him and play a round with him one day. Professional golfer Phil Mickelson seems to be not only a world-class golfer but a great dad as well. It appears that to Phil, being a great dad is more important than just about anything else. I read an article in *Parade Magazine* about him titled, "I Couldn't Be Any Luckier."[95] His devotion to his family moved me, especially through some of the health challenges and losses they endured.

> Mickelson will tell you that his favorite day is one on which he and Amy have a date. "I didn't need all this to happen to know how lucky I am to have her in my life," he says. "She constantly challenges me to be a better person, a better husband, a better father, a better golfer."

> Golf can be a cruel game, but Mickelson has proven his resilience. Case in point: the 2006 U.S. Open at Winged Foot, when he stood on the final tee with a one-shot lead and proceeded to unleash a series of cringeworthy shots

that resulted in a double bogey and cost him the tournament. Sheer agony, but here's Mickelson's story of what happened after: "My daughter Amanda [then 6] and I [found a quiet] corner to snuggle, and she said, 'Are you okay, Dad?' and I said, 'Well, I'm a little disappointed. This was a tournament I dreamed of winning as a kid, and I haven't yet.' And she said, 'Well, second is pretty good, Dad. Can I get you a piece of pizza?'

"It was kind of a bigger-picture perspective," he says, beaming with fatherly pride.

Be a Great Dad Today

Embracing our role and identity as fathers is a choice and a journey that pays a rewarding return on investment. It's worth it for us, and it's worth it for our kids, and their kids, and their kids.

> "When you teach your son, you
> teach your son's son."
> — The Talmud

When we embrace our role and identity as fathers, we will leave a legacy of love and well-being. We'll be better men for it and so thankful we did. We will make progress toward what we really want—to become great dads who enjoy remarkably great relationships with our kids.

Great dads shape great kids. Let's go for it together!

Appendix A:
Action Steps

AN ESSENTIAL STEP in moving from information to transformation is taking action on all the good ideas you've read as well as your own strong desire to become a great dad.

With the worthy goal of real transformation in view, I've gathered together into this appendix all the practical suggestions and ideas I've provided along the way. I suggest keeping a bookmark at this page. By doing so, you can regularly come back to these action steps for inspiration and simple, practical ideas of activities you can do with and for your kids—activities that will help you love and enjoy them, affirm and encourage them, and foster your relationship with them as you shape their character and build their self-esteem, respect, discipline, and security.

Or you can go to our website (www.thegreatdadsproject.org/resources/actionsteps) to download a copy of these to post where you can see them regularly.

Verbal and Written Affirmations:

- ▸ Verbally affirm each of your children every day for something. Catch them doing something right, and then surprise them by telling them you caught them. Specifically name what it is you saw them do or say or decide. Then praise them for it. The Great Dad Challenge™ is designed to help you do this.

- ▸ Write a personal letter to each of your kids, and send it in the mail to them. Tell them in it some of the characteristics you see in them that you admire and appreciate. Tell them how much you love them and how grateful you are that you get to be their dad. Tell them how special they are to you and why.

- ▸ Print something like this below and leave it for them at breakfast one morning (or dinner one evening). Or stick it in their lunch bag so they find it at school. Print this one, or create your own with your own words.

Mom and Dad work hard to provide the money needed to house, feed, clothe, and provide recreation, vacations, and sports opportunities for our family. We do this because we love you so much and value our family time more than anything.

We really appreciate the contributions you each make toward the family's well-being and happiness by doing the household tasks we ask of you. That really helps to make things manageable.

Thank you for all you do.

- ▸ You can write the following affirmation starters on an index card and keep them with you or in the car. Then use them at random times or moments to verbally affirm your children.
  - • One thing I admire most about you is . . .

- One of my favorite memories with you is . . .
- One of the funniest things you have ever done is . . .
- One of my proudest memories of you is . . .
- I like it when you . . .

▸ Dads, we need to tell our daughters and sons:
  - How great we think they are.
  - How proud we are of them.
  - How great we think it is to be their dad.
  - How we wouldn't want any other kid in the world besides them.
  - How lucky we think we are to have the kids we do.
  - How much we love them.

Unconditional and Unending Acceptance:

▸ Print something like this below, and tape it to your children's bedroom wall. Then read it out loud to them.

No matter what you do, no matter where you go, no matter how long it's been, no matter what it costs . . .

As long as I have a penny, you'll never be broke . . .
As long as I have food, you'll never go hungry . . .
As long as I have a coat, you'll never be cold . . .
As long as I have an arm, you'll always be hugged . . .

And if I don't have a penny or food or a coat or if my tired arms are too old to hug any more, then come and stand by my bedside and hold my hand, and know that as long as my heart beats in my body your daddy will always love you!

▸ Consciously think about the difference between approval and acceptance. This is a tricky distinction many dads fail to make. We can disapprove of some action, behavior, or choice our child makes and still express unconditional and unending acceptance of them. That is so much easier said than done. But it is essential to being a great dad and helping our kids feel secure in our loving acceptance. Write down for yourself (without showing it to your kids) what you disapprove of (for example, their hairstyle, a choice of a friend, their music or entertainment, or tantrums they throw), and then write next to each thing of which you disapprove: "But I love and accept you no matter what." Do this as often as you need to in order to remind yourself and to help yourself act and speak in loving and accepting ways to your kids, even while still disapproving of whatever it is you don't like.

Spoken and Physical Affection:

- ▸ Tell each of your kids every day at least once how much you love them and how lucky you feel to be their dad. Then repeat this again in the quiet moments of saying good night at bedtime.
- ▸ Show some sort of appropriate and warm physical affection to each of your kids every day.
  - Give them a hug, a kiss, a pat on the back.
  - Hold their hand.
  - Scoop them up and snuggle them on your lap.
  - Wrestle with them.
  - Stroke or brush their hair.
  - Tickle them.
  - Just get physically close to them and show them your love so they can actually feel it through your body.

Helping Your Kids Feel Your Love:

Here are a few practical suggestions you can use as you practice affirming, accepting, and showing affection to your kids. Try these, and make up your own.

- Tell them daily something you see in them that is positive (affirming something about them). Say it out loud. A spoken affirmation is clear and powerful. If at all possible, touch your kids while you affirm them.

- Tell them every day how much you love them and how glad you are that you are their dad. Something like, "I love you so much, my son/daughter. I'm so happy that you are my child and that I get to be your dad. I love you, and I'm so, so proud of you." If you have a daughter, tell her often how competent and beautiful you think she is and that you'll love her always. Affectionate touch is important. For your son, tell him you're proud of him and believe in him and you'll love him forever.

- For no apparent reason and at seemingly random times, hug them, hold them, and touch them in some appropriate and affectionate, even playful, way to show your love for them and help them *feel* it.

- Affirm them nightly at bedtime, especially when they're young. If you pray, you might pray something like, "May God bless you and keep you and show his great and tender love for you this night, and always. And may his peace be with you. You are my beloved son/daughter, (use your child's name here), and I am so well pleased in you. I will never leave you. I will never forsake you. For you are my son/daughter, and I'll love you forever, no matter what."

- ▸ If you don't pray, you can express the picture you have of a bright future for them and why you see that. Be as specific as you can. Point out and praise character qualities, interests, and skills you see in them and some ways you can imagine them using these to benefit others, perhaps even ways to build a career out of them or start a business. Help them feel the bright picture you have of their future and how proud you are of who they are becoming, what they have accomplished, decisions they've made, and people they've helped.
- ▸ Make the most of special moments in their lives, and make them even more special by adding your affectionate affirmation to the moment.
- ▸ Think deeply about milestone life transitions in your children's lives—rites of passage. Plan a special affirmation for them to mark the occasion and imprint their soul with your delight in them and love for them.

Other Practical Suggestions:

Remember the following suggestions by the first word of each. Use the first letter of each word to spell three trees: a PALM, a FIR, and an OAK.

PALM:

- ▸ **Practice** regularly these action steps.
- ▸ **Attend** live and virtual events with other men on fathering. I'll keep you informed about the ones I present and others I support.
- ▸ **Listen** to inspiring reminders and teaching related to fathering, life transformation, and healing. I do this often while I drive. Get CDs (such as the ones I produce for our Community of Dads, and others), audio messages, podcasts—whatever you can find. I will recommend specific resources for dads to The Community of Dads.

▶ **Meditate** daily on the vision these practices will create in your mind of your best self as a dad. Napoleon Hill, the man Andrew Carnegie commissioned to interview 100 of the world's most successful men and who recorded his observations in his phenomenal bestseller *Think and Grow Rich*, famously asserted, "What the mind can conceive and believe, the mind can achieve." I teach dads how to do this, as I practice it daily myself.

FIR:

▶ **Find** and regularly visit websites such as www.thegreatdad-sproject.org, www.tumblon.com, www.teachinghappiness .com, www.zelawelakids.com, and others, as well as daddy blogs that inspire you toward your goal. See my suggestions on our website under Resources.

▶ **Identify** some potential dad mentors and ask them, one by one, if they will spend some time with you, talk with you about fathering, answer your questions, and help you grow. Get my eBook or audio CD on "Fathering in Community" to learn more about this.

▶ **Read** good books on being a great dad regularly. I help our Community of Dads identify these.

OAK:

▶ **Organize** family goals based on a Great Dad Purpose Statement and review them regularly. Get my eBook or audio CD that teaches dads how to do this: "Craft a Great Dad Purpose Statement."

▶ **Attend** or start a small group with other dads who share your commitment to being the best dad you can be. Get my eBook or audio CD, "Fathering in Community." Then download a sample small group discussion guide from my website (www .thegreatdadsproject.org/resources/smallgroups).

> ▸ **Kraft** a Great Dad Purpose Statement, memorize it, and say it daily to yourself every morning during some quiet, reflective, meditative time. Think of creative ways to live your purpose statement each day in some way. I teach dads how to create their own Great Dad Purpose Statement and why to do so.

Some Great Questions to Ask Your Kids to Generate Conversation:[96]

Fun, get-to-know-them questions:
- ▸ What has been your favorite book? Movie?
- ▸ What's your most prized possession?
- ▸ What's one of your big dreams?
- ▸ What is your favorite meal? Restaurant?
- ▸ If you could travel anywhere, where would you go? And why?
- ▸ If a fire started in our house, what three things would you take out?
- ▸ Who are your top three heroes?
- ▸ When did you have the most fun?
- ▸ If you had $100 to spend, what would you buy?
- ▸ What would you do if you won $1 million?

Some deeper questions that will help you get to know what your child is thinking—who he or she is becoming:
- ▸ What makes you really angry?
- ▸ What embarrasses you? And why?
- ▸ When did you cry the hardest?
- ▸ If you could do three things to change the world, what would they be?
- ▸ What are five things you are really thankful for?
- ▸ What is your greatest fear?
- ▸ What causes you the most stress?
- ▸ Who is your closest friend? Why?

- What three things bug you most about your friends?
- What makes you the happiest?
- What makes you the saddest?
- What was your greatest achievement this last year?
- What was your greatest disappointment this last year?

Helpful, but risky questions to help you be a better parent:
- What do you like to do best with me?
- What do Mom and Dad do that hold you back?
- What do we do that bugs you the most?
- What do you like most about the way Mom is raising you?
- What do you like most about the way Dad is raising you?
- If you could change three things about the way Mom and Dad parent you, what would they be? And why?
- What do you want most from me?

How Do You Stay Focused on Becoming a Great Dad?
- Get ongoing great dad input (join The Great Dads Project Community of Dads).
- Apply regular, helpful practices (PALM, FIR, OAK).
- Follow the action steps given in this appendix.
- Consider personal coaching.
- Accept The Great Dad Challenge™.

Appendix B:
Why Loving Their Mother Means Loving Your Kids

A N EFFECTIVE FATHER who is married knows one important aspect of fathering and loving children will be his relationship with his children's mother. For married men, being a good husband is part of being a great dad. There are numerous studies and books dedicated to the impact of a loving marriage on the healthy development of children. I will simply mention it here. Clinical research indicates kids flourish best when two parents who love each other are involved with and committed to the children they nurture together.[97]

Millions of children will never experience a two-parent family. I didn't. I grew up with a single mom and later a stepdad, and then moved to live with my dad and my stepmother and her four children from two previous marriages. Then my half-brother was born. I experienced the complexities of single-parent and blended families. I don't stand in judgment of men or women who find themselves in a family experience that is not what they had hoped for themselves or for their children.

Dads, we need to know that one of the most important gifts we can give our kids is not only to love them but also to love their moms.[98] If that can mean loving mom and living with her, that's best. But it may also mean showing love to her, even if you don't live together. Showing love in these contexts will look different, but the better your relationship with their mother, the more love your children will feel from you. And the more time you will get with them.[99]

If you are married:

- ▸ Nurture your relationship with your wife.
- ▸ Dedicate time to it.
- ▸ Recognize how fragile relationships can be if you don't protect, guard, and invest in them.
- ▸ Remember special days together—birthdays and anniversaries—and make them special again.
- ▸ Create new special experiences.
- ▸ Date your wife.
- ▸ Listen to her express her heart.
- ▸ Value and prioritize her and help her feel that.

If you're no longer married:

- ▸ Be faithful to pay your financial commitments to your ex-wife without complaint.
- ▸ Speak well of her to your kids.
- ▸ Spend as much time with your children as possible.
- ▸ Call and write often when you're away from them.
- ▸ Offer to relieve their mom whenever she needs a break—if you live close enough to do so.
- ▸ Consistently and creatively apply the practices in this book as much as your situation allows.

Millions of children experience painful and long-lasting consequences of a strained or broken relationship between their moms and dads.[100]

Loving our children means also loving their
mother, whether we're married to her or not.

Loving her may not mean feeling loving
feelings, but it does mean treating
her with love and respect.

Real-Life Example

A few years ago, I met Randy, a dad who still lived with significant childhood wounds. It didn't surprise me that he struggled to put his life together with his wife and two sons. He contacted me and asked for coaching. He wanted to change his life—to treat his wife and children better.

A year after we met, Susan, his wife, secured a restraining order against him due to domestic violence, and he was forced to leave his home and family. I wrote him a letter answering his questions about what he could do now, and when he was allowed to return home. This is part of the letter I sent him.

> Randy, here are four things I try to do for my boys that you might try with yours.
>
> 1. Attend all their sporting events and be supportive, pointing out lots more things they did right (even if you have to make them up) than anything they may have done wrong.
>
> 2. Every day, affirm them at least once (tell them something they did well and that you are proud of

them for) and show some form of affection toward them (hold their hands when walking, have them sit on your lap when reading or watching TV, and kiss them at night/bedtime).

3. When you are back living with them, make a point to tell each of them every day one thing you love about them.

4. Make a few minutes of special time with each one at bedtime. Tell them how much you love them, how glad you are that you get to be their dad, and share with them something you thought about them during the day when you were away from them.

By the way, Randy, you can do these same things for Susan as well. Being a great dad and a great husband involves many of the same kinds of things. I'm proud of you, Randy, for how hard you are working to grow and change. I believe in you. Stay at it, and you will see results.

Much of the ground we covered in this book can also be applied to being a great husband: husbands ought to affirm, accept, and show affection to their wives.

It can also be applied to figuring out how to love the mother of your children even if you are not married to her. Loving the mother of your children, treating her with respect and honor, valuing her and speaking well of her is a vital way to love your kids. You can do this. Make it part of your longing to be a great dad.

Appendix C:
Resources

Books:
You will find reviews of, quotes from, and recommendations of books Keith has read at www.thegreatdadsproject.org/resources/book reviews.

Websites, Blogs, and Forums:
You will find links to useful fathering sites, blogs, and forums Keith recommends at www.thegreatdasdproject.org/resources.

The Great Dads Project: Great Dads Shape Great Kids
www.thegreatdadsproject.org
www.facebook.com/thegreatdadsproject
Twitter: @ForGreatDads

About the Author

KEITH ZAFREN **helps transform fathers into dads.** He is a fathering expert and coach who has learned firsthand how to father. He is an engaging speaker and writer. Keith has been inspiring fathers for 28 years from all walks of life, from executives to inmates, to become the father their children need and want. Through his work as founder of The River Church Community (www.the-river.org), a founding board member and fatherhood trainer for the Prison Entrepreneurship Program (www.pep.org) and Defy Ventures (www.defyventures.org), and now as founder of The Great Dads Project, Keith has touched thousands of lives.

As captain of the rugby team, Keith won an NCAA National Championship at UC Berkley where he graduated with honors and completed his undergraduate and graduate studies in Rhetoric. He earned an M.A. at Asbury Theological Seminary. His personal mission is to relentlessly pursue his own authenticity, healing, and growth, and to create peak experiences that elevate and inspire dads toward self-awareness, receptivity, and transformation through his in-depth research, compelling writing, charismatic speaking, and supportive mentoring.

Keith brings his enthusiasm for personal transformation to dads—and moms—across the country through speaking engagements, workshops, and his new book, *How to Be a Great Dad—No Matter What Kind of Father You Had*. Inspiring his own father journey are his three sons, the healing gifts of his life: JD, Kai, and Cal.

Invite Keith to speak at your event.

Contact Information:

    www.thegreatdadsproject.org

    keith@thegreatdadsproject.org

    Facebook: TheGreatDadsProject

    Twitter: @ForGreatDads

About The Great Dads Project

THE GREAT DADS PROJECT was founded with an inspiring vision that can change the world.

Vision: What We Dream About
To transform millions of fathers into highly effective and deeply fulfilled dads who enjoy great relationships with their kids.

Mission: What We Do
We equip men with the skill set and mindset they need to become the great dads they long to be.

Strategy: How We Accomplish Our Mission
Through inspiration, education, training, and support.

Our Slogan:
Great Dads Shape Great Kids.™ Be a great dad today!

Millions of men long to be better dads, feel close to their kids, and enjoy fathering, but many have experienced inadequate role models, are crippled by their past, father in isolation, and repeat the mistakes their fathers made. Their children pay the price. Dads lack peer support, inspiration, solid training, and mentoring.

The Great Dads Project is changing all that.

Bibliography

Assaraf, John, and Murray Smith. *The Answer: Grow Any Business, Achieve Financial Freedom, and Live an Extraordinary Life.* New York: Atria, 2008.

Canfield, Jack, and Mark Victor Hansen. *Our 101 Best Stories: The Wisdom of Dads; Loving Stories about Fathers and Being a Father.* Chicken Soup for the Soul. Cos Cob, CT: Chicken Soup for the Soul Publishing, 2008.

Canfield, Jack, Mark Victor Hansen, Jeff Aubery, [et all], *Chicken Soup for the Father's Soul: Stories to Open the Hearts and Rekindle the Spirits of Fathers* Chicken Soup for the Soul. Deerfield Beach, Fla: Health Communications, Inc., 2001.

Canfield, Jack, and Janet Switzer. *The Success Principles: How to Get from Where You Are to Where You Want to Be.* New York: Harper, 2005.

Canfield, Ken. *The 7 Secrets of Effective Fathers: Becoming the Father Your Children Need.* Wheaton, IL: Tyndale House Publishers, 1992.

_____. *The Heart of a Father: How You Can Become a Dad of Destiny.* Chicago: Northfield Publishing, 1996, 2006.

Chethik, Neil. *FatherLoss: How Sons of All Ages Come to Terms with the Deaths of Their Dads*. 1st ed. New York: Hyperion, 2001.

Dalbey, Gordon. *Father and Son: The Wound, the Healing, the Call to Manhood*. Nashville: Thomas Nelson Publishers, 1992.

Father Facts 5. National Fatherhood Initiative, 2007.

Glass, Bill, and Terry Pluto. *Champions for Life: The Power of a Father's Blessing*. Deerfield Beach, FL: Faith Communications, 2005.

Guarendi, Ray. *Back to the Family: Proven Advice on Building a Stronger, Healthier, Happier Family*. New York: Villard, 1990.

Haidt, Jonathan. *The Happiness Hypothesis: Finding Modern Truth in Ancient Wisdom*. Cambridge, MA: Basic Books, 2006.

Hamrin, Robert D. *Great Dads: Building Loving Lasting Relationships with Your Kids*. Colorado Springs, CO.: Cook Communications Ministries, 2002.

Heath, Chip, and Dan Heath. *Made to Stick: Why Some Ideas Survive and Others Die*. 1st ed. New York: Random House, 2007.

_____. *Switch: How to Change Things When Change Is Hard*. 1st ed. New York: Broadway Books, 2010.

Hill, Napoleon. *Think and Grow Rich; Teaching, for the First Time, the Famous Andrew Carnegie Formula for Money-Making, Based Upon the Thirteen Proven Steps to Riches*. Meriden, Conn.,: The Ralston society, 1937.

Horn, Wade F., David Blankenhorn, and Mitchell B. Pearlstein, eds. *The Fatherhood Movement: A Call to Action*. Lanham, MD: Lexington Books, 1999.

Hybels, Bill, and LaVonne Neff. *Too Busy Not to Pray : Slowing Down to Be with God*. Downers Grove, IL: InterVarsity Press, 1988.

Joy, Donald. *Unfinished Business: How a Man Can Make Peace with His Past*. Wheaton, IL: Victor Books, 1989.

Katz, David, ed. *Fathers and Sons: 11 Great Writers Talk about Their Dads, Their Boys, and What It Means to Be a Man*. New York: Esquire (Hearst) Books, 2010.

Levine, Suzanne Braun. *Father Courage: What Happens When Men Put Family First*. New York: Harcourt, 2000.

Maslow, Abraham. *Religions, Values, and Peak-Experiences*. New York: Penguin Compass, 1964.

Miller, Donald. *A Million Miles in a Thousand Years: What I learned While Editing My Life*. Nashville: Thomas Nelson, 2009.

_____. *Father Fiction: Chapters for a Fatherless Generation*. Rev. ed. Nashville, Tenn.: Howard Books, 2010.

Miller, Donald, and John MacMurray. *To Own a Dragon: Reflections on Growing Up Without a Father*. Colorado Springs, CO: NavPress, 2006.

Peck, M.D., Scott. *The Road Less Traveled: A New Psychology of Love, Traditional Values, and Spiritual Growth*. New York: Simon and Schuster, 2002.

Pittman, Frank. "Bringing up Father." *Family Therapy Networker*, May/June (1988).

Pruett, M.D., Kyle D. *The Nurturing Father: Journey toward the Complete Man*. New York: Warner Books, 1987.

_____. *Fatherneed: Why Father Care Is as Essential as Mother Care for Your Child*. New York: Broadway Books, 2000.

Scull, Charles, ed. *Fathers, Sons, and Daughters: Exploring Fatherhood, Renewing the Bond*. Los Angeles, CA: Jeremy P. Tarcher, Inc., 1992.

Shapiro, Jerrold Lee. *The Measure of a Man: Becoming the Father You Wish Your Father Had Been*. New York: Delacorte, 1993.

Sheehy, Gail. *Understanding Men's Passages: Discovering the New Map of Men's Lives*. New York: Balllantine Books, 1998.

Sowers, John. *Fatherless Generation: Redeeming the Story*. Grand Rapids, MI: Zondervan, 2010.

Stoop, David. *Making Peace with Your Father: Understanding the Role Your Father Has Played in Your Life—Past to Present*. Ventura, CA: Regal, 1992, 2004.

Trent, John, and Gary Smalley. *The Blessing: Giving the Gift of Unconditional Love and Acceptance*. Nashville: Thomas Nelson, 1993, 2004.

Wade, Dwyane, and Mim Eichler Rivas. *A Father First: How My Life Became Bigger Than Basketball*. 1st ed. New York: William Morrow, 2012.

Wallerstein, Judith S., Julia Lewis, and Sandra Blakeslee. *The Unexpected Legacy of Divorce: A 25 Year Landmark Study*. 1st ed. New York: Hyperion, 2000.

Notes

1   "Our dads were not nearly involved as we are, and it's sort of difficult to figure out what my role is: breadwinner, diaper-changer, benevolent but a distant source of strength. [...] Popular culture isn't much help either. Dads are generally portrayed as complete boneheads." Lawyer Tom Dolgenos quoted in "No Respect: Fathers say their efforts go unappreciated," *The Wall Street Journal*, May 2005.

Suzanne Braun Levine writes, "My most fundamental assumption was that everyone shared an understanding of what fatherhood should be. After all, there are countless studies confirming that where fathers are actively involved in a warm relationship with their children, the children—from premature newborns to preschoolers to adolescents—thrive in childhood and prosper in life. But who needs studies? The expression on a youngster's face at the sight of a beloved dad—and most dads are beloved, even neglectful ones—is study enough. And what about the dad's expression? He would probably be embarrassed to see himself in such a moment of vulnerability and joy, but a snapshot of his face would supersede the mountain of research documenting how fatherhood enriches a man's spirit and brings a special kind of intimacy to his life." Suzanne Braun Levine, *Father Courage: What Happens When Men Put Family First* (New York: Harcourt, 2000), 6. Used by permission.

2   Andrew Merton, "Father Hunger" in Charles Scull, ed. *Fathers, Sons, and Daughters: Exploring Fatherhood, Renewing the Bond* (Los Angeles, CA: Jeremy P. Tarcher, Inc., 1992), 21.

3   This paragraph is adapted from an article in *Christianity Today,* January 2006, Vol. 50, No. 1, p. 48. Interview by Nancy Madsen. Used by permission. Nancy Madsen is a reporter based in Richmond, VA. She may be reached at nancy.madsen@gmail.com.

4   Levine, *Father Courage*, 207.

5   Experts note, "For predicting a child's self-esteem, it is sustained contact with the father that matters for sons, but physical affection from fathers that matters for daughters." Duncan, Greg J., Martha Hill, and W. Jean Yeung. "Fathers' Activities and Children's Attainments." Paper presented at the Conference on Father Involvement, October 10–11, 1996, Washington, D.C., pp. 5–6.

6   Neil Chethik, *FatherLoss: How Sons of All Ages Come to Terms with the Deaths of Their Dads*, 1st ed. (New York: Hyperion, 2001), 255.

7   See Kyle D. Pruett, M.D., *The Nurturing Father: Journey toward the Complete Man* (New York: Warner Books, 1987) and Kyle D. Pruett, M.D., *Fatherneed: Why Father Care Is as Essential as Mother Care for Your Child* (New York: Broadway Books, 2000).

8   Pruett, M.D., *The Nurturing Father*, 18.

9   John Trent and Gary Smalley, *The Blessing: Giving the Gift of Unconditional Love and Acceptance* (Nashville: Thomas Nelson, 1993, 2004), 57.

10 Ray Guarendi, *Back to the Family* (New York: Villard, 1990), 149. Used by permission.

11 An interview with Bill Glass by Nancy Madsen, *Christianity Today,* January 2006, Vol. 50, No. 1, p. 48. Used by permission. Nancy Madsen is a reporter based in Richmond, Virginia. She may be reached at nancy.madsen@gmail.com.

12 "Why was wrestling, lap-sitting, hugging, and other physical affection so fondly remembered by sons? For one thing, it seemed to offer the boy a close-up of the beast he would one day become: a man. The poet Robert Bly, author of *Iron John*, says close contact between a father and son helps the son 'tune' himself to the rhythm of masculinity. The boy experiences, in his body and bones, how a man moves, feels, smells. Just as importantly, according to the sons I spoke with, when the father's touch is playful and loving, the son feels accepted and protected." Chethik, *FatherLoss*, 254.

13 "Affection has the connotation of holding, cuddling, hugging, kissing, and other forms of physical contact. And indeed, when that occurred between a father and son, it seemed to have an unusually positive effect on the child. For many of the sons I spoke with, their fondest memories of childhood were wrestling with their dads, being tossed into the air or carried piggyback, or some other form of direct physical play." Chethik, *FatherLoss*, 253.

14 For more on this, see a delightful essay written by Ron Reagan Jr. about besting his dad, former President Reagan, in a swimming match when he was a teenager. "My Father's Memories" by Ron Reagan in David Katz, ed. *Fathers and Sons: 11 Great Writers Talk about Their Dads, Their Boys, and What It Means to Be a Man*, (New York: Esquire (Hearst) Books, 2010), 113–22.

15 "Nothing scares a dad more than if for any reason he has any sexual feelings towards his daughter," says neuropsychiatrist Dr. Louann Brizendine. "If she comes out in a really hot outfit as she starts to develop and he finds himself reacting a little bit like a guy, he's often just mortified. It's a normal reaction." Quoted online September 2012 in an article titled "Daughter in love; Dad feels jilted" at http://www.cnn.com/2012/07/17/living/jealous-jilted-dad-daughter-in-love/index.html.

16 "Girls who suffered from the denial of positive attention from their fathers in childhood look for him in each relationship they have." Maureen Murdock, "Daughters in the Father's World," in Scull, ed. *Fathers, Sons, and Daughters*, 113.

Also, "Today with the rise in illegitimacy and divorce, fewer fathers are around to protect and defend their daughter's safety and honor. With more girls lacking the love and attention that only a father can give, more of them are willing to settle for perverse alternatives, namely, seeking intimacy with predatory adult men." Gracie S. Hsu, "Leaving the Vulnerable Open to Abuse," *Perspective*, September 9, 1996.

17 In his anthology titled *Fathers, Sons, and Daughters*, psychologist Dr. Charles Scull writes: "A father is the first and often the longest connection a daughter will have with a man. The father-daughter bond (or lack of bond) shapes her future relationships with male friends and lovers and influences how she moves out in the world. If he encourages her efforts to achieve, inspires her budding self-confidence, and teaches her competency skills, she will more easily develop an authentic self-esteem. If he discourages her efforts, undermines her self-confidence, shames her body, or discounts her personal opinions, her self-esteem will be marred, and it may take many years for her to learn to believe in herself." Scull, ed. *Fathers, Sons, and Daughters* , 99.

18 I love how author Neil Chethik puts it. Chethik is writing to dads about their sons, but this could easily translate to daughters as well. "Find reasons to admire him. And every so often, no matter what his age, offer him a gift that can come only from you: Tell him how proud you are to be his dad." This sort of affirming blessing will leave lasting positive marks in a child's life. See Chethik, *FatherLoss*, 267.

19 David Stoop, *Making Peace with Your Father: Understanding the Role Your Father Has Played in Your Life--Past to Present* (Ventura, CA: Regal, 1992, 2004), 73.

20 Donald Miller and John MacMurray Jr., *To Own a Dragon: Reflections on Growing Up Without a Father* (Colorado Springs, CO: NavPress, 2006), 34.

21 Miller and MacMurray, *To Own a Dragon*, 47.

22 The convention was held June 2, 2000. Cited in *Father Facts 5* (National Fatherhood Initiative, 2007), 154.

23 Stoop, *Making Peace with Your Father*, 72.

24 In "Dad's Empty Chair," *New York Times*, July 7, 2005. Cited in *Father Facts 5*, 127.

25 Bill Hybels and LaVonne Neff, *Too Busy Not to Pray: Slowing Down to Be with God* (Downers Grove, IL: InterVarsity Press, 1988), 8.

26 Bill Glass and Terry Pluto, *Champions for Life: The Power of a Father's Blessing* (Deerfield Beach, FL: Faith Communications, 2005), 84.

27 Proverbs 3:27, Jewish scriptures.

28 From *Thoughts From Mike Smith: The Last Word*, an article in HSLDA: The Home School Court Report, Vol. XXVII, No. 2, Mar./Apr. 2011, 46.

29 *Thoughts From Mike Smith* in HSLDA: The Home School Court Report, Vol. XXVII, No. 2, Mar./Apr. 2011, 46.

30 Donald Miller, *A Million Miles in a Thousand Years* (Nashville: Thomas Nelson, 2009), 210–11. Reprinted by permission, Thomas Nelson Inc., Nashville, Tennessee. All rights reserved.

31 Chethik, *FatherLoss*, 258.

32 Stoop, *Making Peace with Your Father*, 139.

33 Stoop, *Making Peace with Your Father*, 139–40.

34 Stoop, *Making Peace with Your Father*, 45.
Later in his book, Stoop writes more regarding a man's relationship with his adolescent son. It's worth noting. "One of a father's most important jobs during his son's adolescence is to challenge him out of the passivity that often dominates a teenage boy's

personality. This is not a minor skirmish. The emotions of the adolescent male are powerful, even explosive, and the battle being fought is a fight between extremes: extreme submissiveness and passivity on the one hand, extreme assertiveness (with an occasional touch of 'I-just-want-to-kill-you' anger) on the other. Living with a male adolescent, and watching the intensity of his emotions as he and his father lock horns, can be quite an experience. And if it is frightening to the observer, it is even more terrifying to the son. A man needs considerable intestinal fortitude to successfully father a boy through this stage of life. Many fathers, though they are still physically present in the family, are too detached or too wishy-washy to stay involved in their son's lives the way they need to be. They abdicate family leadership to the mother and bury themselves in work or some other distraction. Their weakness leads to many of the same results as if they were absent" (135–36).

[35] Stoop, *Making Peace with Your Father*, 45.

[36] Tom Pinkson, "Honoring a Daughter's Emergence into Womanhood" in Scull, ed. *Fathers, Sons, and Daughters*, 148–55 (149).

[37] Evelyn Bassoff, Ph.D., *Cherishing Our Daughters: How Parents Can Raise Girls to Become Strong and Loving Women*, 1998. Cited in *Father Facts 5*, 151.

[38] Gracie S. Hsu, "Leaving the Vulnerable Open to Abuse," *Perspective*, September 9, 1996. Cited in *Father Facts 5*, 151.

[39] Stoop, *Making Peace with Your Father*, 65.

[40] See www.christintherockies.org.

[41] As I thought about what sort of experience I wanted to create for my son, I searched and searched to find examples that might help me. I read books. I searched the Internet. I talked with other dads. I found a few stories about dads who did plan some sort of initiatory experience for their sons. However, I found very little detail explaining how that event took shape and what the dads specifically did with and said to their sons during not just the trip they took but the initiatory "ceremony" part of the experience, if they

included one. For example, Stefan Bechtel writes about his own initiatory canoe and fishing trip he planned for his thirteen-year-old son, Adam, in the Canadian Wilderness. "When I talked to him about some kind of thirteenth-birthday adventure trip, he told me that what he really wanted was to walk to the bottom of the Grand Canyon and back. He basically wanted bragging rights to a good story. But I really preferred something slower and quieter; I wanted to show him the wilderness without having to prove anything to anybody. But most of all I wanted to reacquaint myself with my son, whom—in the bustle of boyhood, Smashing Pumpkins, Nintendo, backward ball caps, and all the rest of it—I seemed to have lost. He was passing from the sweet vulnerability of childhood to the hulking sullenness of adolescence so fast, I sometimes imagined I'd wake up to discover he'd grown a full beard overnight.

"Like many fathers of my generation and my culture, I also longed for some sort of celebration, some rite of passage that would clearly delineate my son's child-self from his impending man-self—preferably an event more spiritual than getting a driver's license and less painful than circumcision.

"We settled on a canoe trip. To my relief, my worries about having nothing to say to each other proved absurd. In fact, he seemed almost as famished for my company as I was for his. I rediscovered the delightfully daft and ingenious mind I remembered him having from his childhood."

Bechtel describes their threatening experience going over some rapids, being capsized, and surviving together. He draws some good lessons learned. But he writes nothing of any celebration specifically, nor any words of blessing he spoke to Adam. It was all about the canoe experience. Great stuff, but I wanted and needed more. Jack Canfield et al. *Chicken Soup for the Father's Soul: Stories to Open the Hearts and Rekindle the Spirits of Fathers*, Chicken Soup for the Soul (Deerfield Beach, FL: Health Communications, Inc., 2001), 20.

[42] Trent and Smalley, *The Blessing*, 76.

[43] Chethik, *FatherLoss*, 258.

44 Chethik, *FatherLoss*, 258–59.

45 Found December, 19, 2011 at http://fatherapprentice.com/2010/good-enough-is-good-enough. Emphasis his.

46 Reported in *John Sowers, Fatherless Generation: Redeeming the Story* (Grand Rapids, MI: Zondervan, 2010), 36–37.

47 Cited in Pruett, M.D., *Fatherneed*, 38.

48 Cited in Gail Sheehy, *Understanding Men's Passages: Discovering the New Map of Men's Lives* (New York: Balllantine Books, 1998), 166. Emphasis hers.

49 Sheehy, *Understanding Men's Passages*, 166.

50 From the *Introduction to Section II: Father and Son – the Search* by Charles Scull in Scull, ed. *Fathers, Sons, and Daughters*, 53.

51 Ken Canfield, *The Heart of a Father: How You Can Become a Dad of Destiny* (Chicago: Northfield Publishing, 1996, 2006), 22.

52 Scull, ed. *Fathers, Sons, and Daughters*, 214.
Also, Gary Oliver, coauthor of *Raising Sons and Loving It*, writes, "In more than 25 years of working with men, I've found one of the biggest roadblocks to becoming whole and healthy is dealing with the deep wounds and hurts from their relationship with their dad." Mark Crawford, author and psychologist, writes, "Whether they were active or absent, our fathers played a vital role in shaping who we are. For many, Dad's influence was a painful one." Both quotes are endorsements cited for Stoop, *Making Peace with Your Father*, endorsements page.

53 "Those of us who remain unaware of the personal hurts and rejections of our boyhoods will tend unconsciously to pass them on to our children. Introspection and awareness of our personal motivations and history are prerequisites to good fathering." Jerrold Lee Shapiro, *The Measure of a Man: Becoming the Father You Wish Your Father Had Been* (New York: Delacorte, 1993), 5.

54 From *Midlife Reconciliation with the Father* by Alan Javurek in Scull, ed. *Fathers, Sons, and Daughters*, 222.

55 "Your personal history as a son has set examples and challenges for you as a father. Your abilities to tolerate ambiguity, to express your emotions, to be patient, and to be empathic will influence your fathering. Wishing to be a certain kind of dad is a good start. Knowing how you were fathered and how you have developed as a man will constitute a next step." Shapiro, *The Measure of a Man*, 134.

56 "Dr. Pittman argues that fatherless men, lacking a male model of fathering, may go through life in a 'childlike' way. Men raised exclusively by women naturally expect that both they and their children will be cared for by their wives. They may have no real idea of what is expected of an adult man in return. 'Men who have been raised without fathers can't help but be amateur parents, and may even be amateur human beings.'" Shapiro, *The Measure of a Man*, 156.

57 Fred Gustafson explains further, "In today's culture, the father-son relationship is in terrible condition. It is both wounded and wounding. It is armored with a rage that rarely gets defined and tightly conceals a pain and a sadness that, once touched, usually brings tears or uncontrolled weeping. When the father-son bond is not intact in a way that nourishes the son's growth, and when the father does not act as a vehicle for transmitting some of the masculine mysteries to the son, that child will grow up with a limited and crippling sense of his masculinity." From "Fathers, Sons, and Brotherhood" by Fred Gustafson in Scull, ed. *Fathers, Sons, and Daughters*, 72.

58 Donald Joy, *Unfinished Business: How a Man Can Make Peace with His Past* (Wheaton, IL: Victor Books, 1989), 47.

59 "Men who grew up without a close connection with their own father may be prone to replicating that low level of involvement. Or if that experience was particularly painful to them, they may do just the opposite. Certainly if you were abused or abandoned as a child, you will have more to overcome in order to be close to your own children. Similarly, men whose own psyche is damaged

and those who suffer from low self-esteem may have more trouble being involved fathers." Shapiro, *The Measure of a Man*, 133.

60 "Children with father wounds are everywhere—surely many of us. They're easy to spot. Without the heart in their day-to-day living, without the color of feelings, life is drab. They can go to all the right parties in all the right clothes and still never have a good time. Pervading their lives is a lack of élan, a theme of melancholy—regret, despair even—that underlies their apparently successful life stories. The spark is missing. Since many more children now grow up without fathers or with part-time fathers only, whether because of divorce or because many men devote so much of their time to work and other activities rather than to fathering, the number of adult children of absentee fathers is astronomical and growing higher daily." Scull, ed. *Fathers, Sons, and Daughters*, 214.

61 "Whether we think of that damage as being to the 'inner child of the past,' or the 'figurine within,' or as a 'hole in the soul,' the painful imagery tells it all. The damage is early and deep, and is the root of symptoms he will bear in the adolescent and adult years. Most of these disappointing fathers were themselves damaged in their childhood. At some level the wounded sons and the damaged fathers are both victims. But we can trace this "unfinished business" with fathers, typically, across four or five generations before the dramatic effects begin to fade." Joy, *Unfinished Business*, 49.

62 From the *Introduction to Section V: Renewing the Bond: Healing Within and Without* by Charles Scull in Scull, ed. *Fathers, Sons, and Daughters*, 207.

63 Joy, *Unfinished Business*, 35.

64 "The abandoned son will have to find some way to explain to himself why his father left. His personal explanations of the abandonment may involve magical feelings of omnipotence (e.g., "I drove him away because I was too bad, too powerful," etc.) or impotence (e.g., "he left because I was a disappointment"). Both the omnipotent and

impotent feelings come from the childlike (superstitious) thinking of overresponsibility. Once internalized, the feeling of having caused the father's absence can become the source of two divergent feelings in later life: (1) deep loneliness, disconnection, and sense of isolation and (2) guilt (at having caused the absence). Each of these may have dramatic impact on later personal self-esteem and on intimate relationships. A son without an internalized sense of a real father will try to explain the absence to himself. There is fertile ground for fabrication. Commonly these sons either idealize or degrade the father, identify with the fantasy, and then struggle with the shame or guilt. As an adult he may well fear another abandonment to the point of being afraid of relationships, avoiding showing vulnerable feelings, or becoming overly dependent on a woman to avoid rejection." Shapiro, *The Measure of a Man*, 185–86.

65 "Research indicates children have a tendency to blame themselves for their parents' divorce: 'If I had only been a better kid, then Mom and Dad wouldn't be upset, and Dad wouldn't have left.' In an even greater leap of logic, children also occasionally blame themselves for their father's death. If you are a fatherless child, you are not responsible for your fatherlessness." Canfield, *The Heart of a Father*, 64.

66 Shapiro, *The Measure of a Man*, 157.

67 "The most visible symptom [of what Dan Kiley calls *the Peter Pan Syndrome*] is their social paralysis. These Peter Pans seem unable to enter into full adult male responsibility—a subtle point made in the Peter Pan musical where the part requires a young woman to play the Peter role, in an effort to show a 'Boy' with unchanged voice and childhood preoccupations. These 'Peter Pan' adult men suffer from shattered self-respect, insecurity from watching an unpredictable father, and feelings of having been betrayed by him. All of this has damaged the sense of self." Joy, *Unfinished Business*, 48.

[68] Scull, ed. *Fathers, Sons, and Daughters*, 215.

[69] Donald Miller, *Father Fiction: Chapters for a Fatherless Generation*, Rev. ed. (Nashville, TN.: Howard Books, 2010), 37. Reprinted with permission of Howard Books, a Division of Simon & Schuster, Inc. from *FATHER FICTION: Chapters for a Fatherless Generation* by Donald Miller. Copyright © 2010 Donald Miller.

[70] Miller, *Father Fiction*, 38. Reprinted with permission of Howard Books, a Division of Simon & Schuster, Inc. from *FATHER FICTION: Chapters for a Fatherless Generation* by Donald Miller. Copyright © 2010 Donald Miller.

[71] "Several studies do indicate that males with absent fathers or father substitutes never quite grow into their own manhood. Psychologically they remain adolescents, have difficultly with commitments, tend to reject masculine values, and have an incomplete sense of exploration or self-affirmation. In his absence a boy may be more inclined toward hero worship and media images of men. Inappropriate images of heroic men in popular media may mislead a boy into excessive aggressiveness, exclusive orientation to winning, or a superficial sense of manhood." Shapiro, *The Measure of a Man*, 227–28.

[72] Canfield, *The Heart of a Father*, 47.

[73] From the *Introduction to Section V: Renewing the Bond: Healing Within and Without* by Charles Scull in Scull, ed. *Fathers, Sons, and Daughters*, 208.

[74] Frank Pittman, "Bringing Up Father," *Family Therapy Networker* May/June (1988): 22.

[75] Sheehy, *Understanding Men's Passages*, 166.

[76] Charles Scull writes, "Forgiving our fathers allows us to stop closing our hearts to them. Ultimately, healing is coming home to feeling fullness and preciousness in our hearts. Giving our offspring what we didn't receive is a wonderful way to heal our own wounds." From the *Introduction to Section V: Renewing the Bond: Healing Within and Without* by Charles Scull in Scull, ed. *Fathers, Sons, and Daughters*, 209.

77 "To some extent a therapist can provide some of that deficient parenting. More significantly, the therapist can provide an environment for the father to find ways of parenting himself, to accept himself for who he is, and to mature psychologically." Shapiro, *The Measure of a Man*, 250.

78 "For most of us help from a guide, mentor, or psychotherapist makes this internal journey go faster and more effectively. To choose the struggle and face the fear of the unknown is an arduous journey. The alternative is to unknowingly replicate our own hurts upon our children—an unfair, unreasonable, and ungrowthful enterprise." Shapiro, *The Measure of a Man*, 218.

79 E.g., "For me to be successful in a long-term intimate relationship, and to be a good father myself, I will need to reconnect with my father and what he represents for me. It is through him, and my internal image of him, that I may pick up the missing threads of my heritage, my masculinity, and my emotional birthright. With a fuller awareness of my history and my fathering, I will be more aware of what it is I offer my future partner or children. To be the kind of man, partner, and father I want to be, I need to better understand who I am inside, and the path to that awareness runs right through my father's house." Shapiro, *The Measure of a Man*, 208.

80 I am indebted to Dan and Chip Heath for the idea of making ideas *stick* (that is, causing them to be memorable in a way that produces change). See Chip Heath and Dan Heath, *Made to Stick: Why Some Ideas Survive and Others Die.* 1st ed. (New York: Random House, 2007).

81 "Freud, Plato, and Buddha all lived in worlds full of domesticated animals. They were familiar with the struggle to assert one's will over a creature much larger than the self. But as the twentieth century wore on, cars replaced horses, and technology gave people ever more control over their physical worlds. When people looked for metaphors, they saw the mind as the driver of a car, or as a program running on a computer. It became possible to forget all about Freud's unconscious, and just study the mechanisms of

thinking and decision making. That's what social scientists did in the last third of the century: Social psychologists created 'information processing' theories to explain everything from prejudice to friendship. Economists created 'rational choices' models to explain why people do what they do. The social sciences were uniting under the idea that people are rational agents who set goals and pursue them intelligently by using the information and resources at their disposal. But then, why do people keep doing such stupid things? Why do they fail to control themselves and continue to do what they know is not good for them?" Jonathan Haidt, *The Happiness Hypothesis: Finding Modern Truth in Ancient Wisdom* (Cambridge, MA: Basic Books, 2006), 3.

Haidt offers an intriguing analogy of an elephant and a rider to represent our powerful subconscious beliefs and desires versus our rational decision-making consciousness. This metaphor is picked up by the Heath brothers and used masterfully in their book on change theory: Chip Heath and Dan Heath, *Switch: How to Change Things When Change Is Hard*, 1st ed. (New York: Broadway Books, 2010).

[82] Dan and Chip Heath make extensive and provocative use of Haidt's metaphor in their book on change. See Heath and Heath, *Switch*.

[83] Haidt, *The Happiness Hypothesis*, 17.

[84] Haidt, *The Happiness Hypothesis*, 21.

[85] Haidt, *The Happiness Hypothesis*, 26. Emphasis mine. See also Heath and Heath, *Switch*.

[86] Abraham Maslow, *Religions, Values, and Peak-Experiences* (New York: Penguin Compass, 1964), 29.

[87] Pruett, M.D., *The Nurturing Father*, 282.

[88] Questions from Shapiro, *The Measure of a Man*.

[89] Lucius Annaeus Seneca (c. 4 B.C.E.—A.D. 65), Roman orator, philosopher and playwright, tutor and advisor of Emperor Nero.

[90] Proverbs 10:12, Jewish scriptures.

91 Cited In Jack Canfield and Mark Victor Hansen, *Our 101 Best Stories: The Wisdom of Dads; Loving Stories About Fathers and Being a Father*, Chicken Soup for the Soul (Cos Cob, CT: Chicken Soup for the Soul Publishing, 2008), 179.

92 Levine, *Father Courage*, Preface, xx. Used by permission.

93 Levine, *Father Courage*, 176. Used by permission.

94 Shapiro, *The Measure of a Man*, 123.

Shapiro adds, "Strong, self-assured, knowledgeable, protective, fair, worthy of respect, willing to take appropriate risks—these are all descriptive of traditional fathering. They remain a cornerstone of good fathering. To these must be added nurturance, sensitivity to children's age-appropriate needs, effective listening, access to and expression of emotions, humor, willingness to work on the marital relationship, self-awareness, and increased time with the family. Children with such a father may expand their sense of manhood to include many traits that are often considered exclusively maternal. Such an expanded notion of gender roles allows both sons and daughters greater freedom in developing their own unique ways in their world." Shapiro, *The Measure of a Man*, 147.

95 Printed in *Parade*, March 27, 2011, in the *Lexington Herald-Leader* Sunday newspaper.

96 I have adapted and revised these questions from Robert D. Hamrin, *Great Dads: Building Loving Lasting Relationships with Your Kids* (Colorado Springs, CO: Cook Communications Ministries, 2002) and Canfield, *The Heart of a Father* .

97 The Case for Marriage Education and Responsible Fatherhood:

> ▸ The best predictor of father presence is marital status; when a father's romantic relationship with the child's mother ends, more likely than not, so does the involvement with their children.[1]

> ▸ Researchers have found a positive correlation between marital quality and the quality of the father-child relationship[2] as well as his competence as a parent.[3]

▸ When marital conflict is high, fathers have a more difficult time being involved with their children, which weakens the father-child relationship.[4]

▸ Researchers found evidence to support the view that marriage confers advantage in terms of father involvement above and beyond the characteristics of the fathers themselves, whereas biology does not.[5]

▸ Researchers concluded that strengthening the inter-parental relationship can support quality fathering.[6]

Found May 5, 2011 at http://highplainscoalition.com/research-impact-on-society-responsible-fatherhood. All of the above data is documented with bibliographic notes not included here (though indicated by the note references left intact). Sources can be found on the site.

[98] Gordon Dalbey shares some wisdom for dads in a book he wrote about fathers and sons, so he speaks explicitly of what a man can give his son, but it is equally true for daughters. He writes, "One major gift a man can give his son is to be present to his mother emotionally as well as physically, to respect her feelings and stand by her . . ." Gordon Dalbey, *Father and Son: The Wound, the Healing, the Call to Manhood* (Nashville: Thomas Nelson Publishers, 1992), 47.

Charles Ballard is the President of the Institute for Responsible Fatherhood and Family Revitalization, which he began in Cleveland in 1978 to work with teen fathers. Ballard "is not merely moralizing or engaging in sentimentality when he says that the most important job of a father is to 'love the mother of his child' and the most important job of employees of his Institute for Responsible Fatherhood is to 'model excellence in marriage.'" Wade F. Horn, David Blankenhorn, and Mitchell B. Pearlstein, eds., *The Fatherhood Movement: A Call to Action* (Lanham, MD: Lexington Books, 1999), xiv–xv.

[99] Ken Canfield devotes an entire chapter in one of his books on being a great dad to "Loving Their Mother." He writes, "A strong marriage

does much to help you fulfill your fathering role." Then he speaks directly to dads and asks, "Do you love your kids? Well, one of the best things you can do for them is to love their mother. The main benefit to your children of good marital interaction between you and your wife is an atmosphere of security." He is sensitive to the many dads who no longer are married to their kids' mom, or do not live with their children, but he is also clear that kids do better when mom and dad live together and love each other (and cites numerous studies to support his conclusion). Ken Canfield, *The 7 Secrets of Effective Fathers: Becoming the Father Your Children Need* (Wheaton, IL: Tyndale House Publishers, 1992), 131ff.

[100] See the landmark study by Judith S. Wallerstein, Julia Lewis, and Sandra Blakeslee, *The Unexpected Legacy of Divorce: A 25 Year Landmark Study*, 1st ed. (New York: Hyperion, 2000).